PRESIDENTIAL SCANDALS

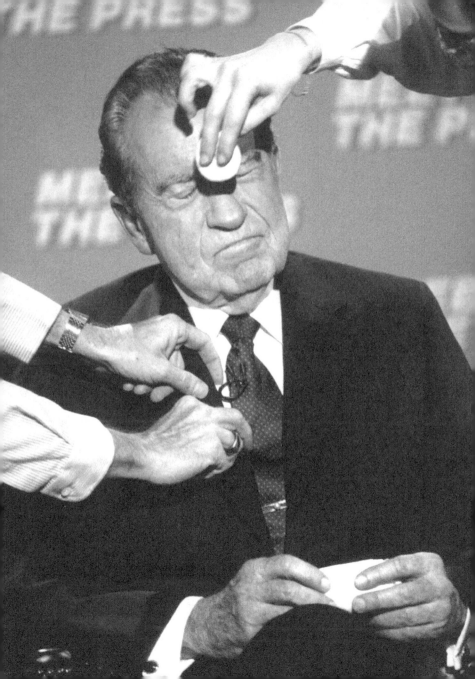

PRESIDENTIAL
SCANDALS

JEFFERSON TO OBAMA

LIGHTNING
GUIDES

Bradford WG Public Library
425 Holland St. W.
Bradford, ON L3Z 0J2

ISBN Print: 978-1-942411-58-1
eBook: 978-1-942411-59-8

"The truth is that all men having power ought to be mistrusted."

—JAMES MADISON

Compared to the scandals and controversies of those that held the office before him, Barack Obama is a boring President. Even his nickname, "No Drama Obama," underlines the paucity of scandal his administration has brought to the White House. His handling of the 2012 Benghazi crisis—after Islamic militants attacked the American diplomatic compound in Libya, the US State Department was criticized for denying requests for extra consulate security— came close. But even Obama's politically motivated opponents seem unsure whether to lay the tragedy at his feet or those of his previous Secretary of State (and 2016 presidential candidate) Hillary Clinton.

Prior heads of state came with headlines, whispers, and accusations of everything from alcoholism to patronage to treason. Scandal, especially at the highest level of power, is as nuanced as it is absolute. For example, JFK's very public infidelities were scurrilous. George W. Bush's concepts of unilateralism, preemptive war and executive privilege were even questioned by those in his own party—a glaring irony considering that many of Bush's scandals had Republican ideological origins. Even George Washington's patriotism was challenged when he granted Britain a highly favored form of trade status shortly after the Revolutionary War, in which redcoats slaughtered Americans by the tens of thousands—a scandal born of political pragmatism.

Washington began his term ready to make necessary self-sacrifices as the president. The day he left his home for the official office, he wrote,

> About ten o'clock, I bade adieu to Mount Vernon, to private life, and to domestic felicity and, with a mind oppressed with more anxious and painful sensations than I have words to express, set out for New York . . . to render service to my country in obedience to its call, but with less hope of answering its expectations.

Forty-three men have answered the presidency's call since Washington's response in 1789. All have suffered public scrutiny, critique, and scandal—all have been found wanting by some part of an increasingly demanding American public. To the president is credited all of the glory and might of a powerful nation, and projected onto him are all of the nation's deficits, controversies, and defeats.

CONTENTS

first, a few facts

Thomas Jefferson helped popularize French dining in America after having his head chef professionally trained in France

HERBERT HOOVER BECAME AN ORPHAN AT AGE NINE

WOODROW WILSON EXTENDED SEGREGATION TO THE WHITE HOUSE

George H. W. Bush celebrated his 75th, 80th, 85th, and 90th birthdays by skydiving

Andrew Jackson, estimated to have participated in upwards of 100 duels, carried a bullet in his chest for his entire presidency

How many Presidents are known to have had extra-marital affairs?

Probably more than anyone can confirm. Thomas Jefferson had an inappropriate relationship with his fourteen-year-old slave Sally Hemings and fathered six of her children. Warren Harding was rumored to have been blackmailed (upon his nomination for Presidency) by Carrie Fulton Phillips, his former lover. James Garfield admitted to having an affair with Lucia Calhoun. Franklin D. Roosevelt had a long affair with Lucy Mercer, who was by his side even on his deathbed. Dwight D. Eisenhower fell for his driver (and former model), Kay Summersby. Lyndon B. Johnson was rumored to have affairs with Madeleine Brown and Alice Glass. And there are numerous stories associated with John F. Kennedy and Bill Clinton.

Have all administrations been marred by scandal?

To a lesser or greater extent, yes, though (of course) not all scandals were the same. John Quincy Adams was attacked as a monarchist because his father was also president. Teddy Roosevelt's opponents sought to discredit his policies and administration because of his desire to overturn the traditional power structure in the Republican Party. President Taft, though well liked and considered an all around congenial person, was dogged by commentary related to his size—his weight often fluctuated between 255 and 350 pounds.

What was the first Presidential scandal?

Jay's Treaty (1794) gave Great Britain favored-nation trade status in exchange for pulling British troops out of forts across the West. The Jeffersonian party of Congress reacted violently and Thomas Jefferson repeatedly accused George Washington of treason. So began a long history of scandal in the executive branch.

Who was the only president to resign from office?

Richard Nixon resigned from office in 1974 when it became evident that audiotapes tied him to "Watergate," the criminal conspiracy to steal information from the Democratic National Party. A united Congress was set to impeach Nixon; however, he resigned before the House voted on the Articles of Impeachment. Despite his resignation, Nixon never admitted wrongdoing and was preemptively pardoned by his successor, President Gerald Ford.

How many presidents have been impeached?

Two presidents have been impeached while in office; neither was convicted of the charges filed against him. The first was Andrew Johnson. Johnson was accused of violating the Tenure of Office Act, which required that a president gain Senate approval before he could remove any of his Congress-confirmed Cabinet members. The second was Bill Clinton, who was impeached on two charges—one count of perjury, and one of obstruction of justice in connection with the Monica Lewinsky scandal.

How many Presidents have been divorced?

There has been one divorcee president and two widower presidents in American history. Ronald Reagan divorced his first wife, Jane Wyman, in 1948, well before his presidency. John Tyler and Woodrow Wilson both became widowers during their tenure.

SETTING THE TONE

SQUABBLES OF POWER AND PUBLIC RELATIONS

George Washington and John Adams—credited with creating the foundation of what we now know as the United States of America—left behind powerful legacies. Despite their historical lionization, the two did not lack for controversy in their own times. Washington was all but accused of cowardice by several senior members of his military Cabinet. Adams had an imperious streak, was fond of grandiose titles, and believed in a Federalist system some have described as close to monarchy.

THE FATHER OF THE NATION

Well before he took office, during his now historic run as the Commander in Chief of the Continental Army of the United States, George Washington was already embroiled in scandal. In 1777 a group of senior Continental Army officers called the "Conway Cabal" (after General Thomas Conway, an Irish mercenary vying for higher office) tried to have Washington replaced as Commander in Chief. Among the group were Samuel Adams, noted American statesman and brewer; Benjamin Rush, one of the leaders of the American Enlightenment; and Thomas Mifflin, merchant and politician.

Angered by the loss of the city of Philadelphia to British forces under Washington's command, Conway wrote a letter to fellow General Horatio Gates, saying "Heaven has been determined to save your Country; or a weak General and bad Counsellors would have ruined it." After hearing of the letter, Washington confronted Conway, who admitted to writing the correspondence but not to criticizing the general. Perceiving criticism among his ranks a great offence and threat to the revolutionary cause, Washington sent a letter to Congress emphasizing the importance of having a united army in what was already a difficult war for the States.

The members of the Cabal appealed to Congress to clear their names and declared their loyalty to Washington, saying that they could not, and would never, conceive of another Commander for the United Forces. In the ensuing years, Thomas Mifflin, James Wilkinson, and Thomas Conway all resigned their positions in the army. Years later, Washington would still face criticism for what was viewed as weakness in his dealings with the British. Jay's Treaty, an agreement between Great Britain and the newly formed United States of America, was signed in 1794—much to the dismay of Thomas Jefferson and the Republican Party.

[
Silas Deane was sent to France by Congress to convince the French government to help the colonies. However, Deane recruited mercenary officers that proved to be liabilities. Among them was General Thomas Conway.
]

The treaty, still considered one of the most controversial to ever be put before the Senate, attempted to resolve the differences between the United States and Britain over trade restrictions. In return for pulling their troops out of forts in what was then considered the Northwest Territory (present day western Pennsylvania and north of the Ohio River) and compensating the States for seized merchant ships, the British were given favored-nation trade status, or low tariffs and high import quotas in the United States. The party viewed Washington as a traitor for this pact, and many considered Jay's Treaty a humiliation to the United States. When news of the treaty became public, mobs took to the streets condemning Washington for supporting the treaty, and the Senate for ratifying it. Effigies of John Jay, the statesman who bargained the deal, were burned in the streets. In New York, Alexander Hamilton, an avid supporter of the treaty, was stoned by a mob.

While most of the criticism surrounding Washington was more ideological and political in nature, the second President of the United States, John Adams, started his tenure off by personally offending more than a few citizens.

HIS ROTUNDITY

John Adams was elected as the second President of the United States in 1796, winning a narrow victory over his bitter rival Thomas Jefferson. The two had been friends and colleagues during the drafting of the Declaration of Independence, but became ideological enemies over a disagreement about the proper size and function of the federal government—a debate that also inspired the formation of the first political

DID YOU KNOW

George Washington's supporters liked to compare him to classical Roman leaders. He was nicknamed "The American Fabius" after a general who avoided large battles to engage in smaller ones. He was also called "The American Cincinnatus" after another Roman (pictured below) who chose a private life instead of using his fame for personal reward.

parties. Adams aligned himself with the Federalists, favoring stronger government, while Jefferson argued for the Democratic-Republicans, favoring limited federal power. Soon after taking office, Adams also entered into a heavy month-long debate in the Senate over the official title of the president.

A direct descendant of the Puritan colonists, Adams studied at Harvard University, served in the First Continental Congress and as Washington's vice president. Adams' education and previous positions, combined with his conservative and religious background, led him to prefer grandiose titles such as "His Majesty the President," echoing the labels of British monarchy. Many Senate members (wanting to distance themselves from the oppressive power structures of the European states) favored the plain, "President of the United States." As such, Adams was perceived as pompous for preferring titles that echoed royalty. He was also critiqued for his size. In jest, Adams' critics later nicknamed him "His Rotundity." This title would not be the end of Adams' embarrassments.

NOT SO NEUTRAL

Despite America's Proclamation of Neutrality (1793), war between France and Britain began to affect American interests quite early in Adams' term. The British and French navies both saw outside trade relations with America as support for the enemy and strategically began seizing American ships and pirating enemy supplies. Adams found himself in a difficult position. As president, he needed to respond to the aggression but did not want to end up in another war. With American unrest growing, Adams wasted no time in applying his ideological preferences through the exercise of power. In an effort to strengthen Federalism and national security, Adams helped pass the Alien and Sedition Acts. These four bills increased the residency requirements for US citizenship, restricted speech that was critical of the federal government, and allowed the president to deport foreigners considered "dangerous to the peace and safety of the United States."

While an astute political move, the acts also served to popularly identify the Federalists as pro-British monarchists and Republicans as pro-French republicans. Jefferson took advantage of this association when an Adams-appointed peace commission (Charles Cotesworth Pinckney, John Marshall, and Elbridge Gerry) failed to meet with the French government. The commission derailed largely over a cultural misunderstanding.

In Europe, it was a fairly common practice for minor officials to solicit bribes on behalf of their bosses in order to gain access to higher-level staff. However, the Americans were appalled when proxies of French Foreign Minister Talleyrand requested $250,000. The Americans insulted the French commission by flat out refusing to even consider the exchange of money.

Pinckney, Marshall, and Gerry left Europe empty-handed and

the Americans had no choice but to build up their navy and send them in search of retribution against the British and French. Thus began the "Quasi-War" in 1798 in which American and French war frigates engaged in skirmishes in the Caribbean for the next two years. A formal treaty was signed in 1800 ending hostilities. However, by that time, Adams' reputation was tarnished: he had been unable to avert war and had failed diplomatically.

The XYZ Affair—XYZ was used to reference Hottinguer (X), Bellamy (Y), and Hauteval (Z), French diplomats left unnamed in documents describing the conflicts between France and the United States—led to the establishment of the United States Marine Corps and the United States Navy. In tandem with XYZ, the Alien and Sedition acts fueled opposition to the Federalist Party and ultimately led to Adams' defeat by Jefferson in the election of 1800.

By the time Adams left office, a template had been created that all future presidents would, in one way or another, experience. Opposition parties would be free to critique, undermine, and oppose administration policy and, from the public's standpoint, the president would largely be held accountable for the nation's failures, be they real, perceived, or manufactured.

TESTING TAXATION

WHISKEY AND THE FEDERAL GOVERNMENT

President Washington had trouble convincing the newly established citizens of the United States to pay taxes to the government. After Treasury Secretary Alexander Hamilton's "whiskey tax" became law in 1791, most distillers openly refused to pay collectors. Traditionally, excess corn and wheat was distilled into whiskey and used as a form of currency on the frontier. The issue came to a head when more than 500 armed men attacked the Pennsylvania home of General John Neville in protest. Washington, a sitting president, called for state governors to raise militia and personally led 13,000 men to quell the insurgency.

Played out as the overreach of the federal government, distillers in Kentucky resisted paying the excise for more than six years after The Whiskey Rebellion. The first tax imposed on a domestic product, "whiskey tax" rhetoric still echoes in present day policy.

CRIMES OF PASSION

JEFFERSON'S APPETITES, PERSONAL AND POLITICAL

Describing Thomas Jefferson without footnoting a large portion of US history is nigh impossible. He served as the principle author of the Declaration of Independence, the third President of the United States, and was an effective proponent of Republicanism. Jefferson also oversaw the Louisiana Purchase from France in 1803 and sent Lewis and Clark on their famous expedition to explore the New West, effectively doubling the size of the United States during his presidency.

Above: Illustration of the Duel Between Alexander Hamilton and Aaron Burr.

That said, Jefferson's vice presidential pick, Aaron Burr, would be charged with murder while in office and later attempt to make war on the United States. However, Jefferson was also no angel. If held to contemporary standards, he would be have been convicted as a pedophile and rapist.

THE BURR DEBACLE

Jefferson and Aaron Burr competed for ballot votes in the presidential election of 1800. When Jefferson won the presidency he took Burr as his Vice President, as was customary at the time. Burr had a history of contention with those in Washington, however, especially with Alexander Hamilton. The two had their political disagreements: Burr was a Republican and advocated for limited government while Hamilton was a Federalist and argued for more power consolidated in the state.

In 1791 Burr won a United States Senate seat from Philip Schuyler, Hamilton's father-in-law. This angered Hamilton, who would have counted on Schuyler's support for his public and economic policies. Instead, Hamilton was forced to engage with Burr, who countered and obstructed his every move.

When Burr ran for New York governor in 1804, Hamilton lobbied against him and Burr, consequently, suffered a landslide defeat. After Hamilton's cutting remarks on Burr's character were published in the Albany Register newspaper, the acrimony came to a head and Burr invited Hamilton to a duel.

Early on the morning of July 11, 1804, Burr and Hamilton met at Weehawken, New Jersey, on a secluded grassy ledge along the Hudson River. Burr mortally wounded Hamilton that morning. Hamilton died the next day. Ironically, he had previously passed

legislation making dueling illegal in the state of New York, as tragically, his own son had been killed in a duel in the same spot two years earlier.

Burr, technically still the vice president, was indicted for the murder of Alexander Hamilton, in addition to the misdemeanor of challenging to a duel. Burr fled—first to New Jersey, where he was soon indicted for murder as well. He went as far as the duel-friendly state of Georgia to avoid conviction, effectively ending his political career. No pardon was forthcoming from the president.

Burr eventually traveled west where he conspired to start a war between the United States and Spain in order to claim land for himself in the ensuing struggle. His co-conspirator, General James Wilkinson, exposed Burr's conspiracy to the White House. None other than President Jefferson issued a warrant for Burr's arrest. Despite Jefferson using all of his political clout to find a conviction, his case against Burr would not stick. Ultimately, a lack of evidence led to Burr's acquittal. Afterwards, Burr fled to Europe, never to appear in the public eye again.

EXECUTIVE OVERREACH

Though he publically condemned the use of federal power, Jefferson was not above the application of it himself. He became personally embroiled in controversy over the impeachment of Federalist John Pickering, New Hampshire Superior Court Chief Justice and United States District Court of New Hampshire judge.

There had been many complaints concerning Pickering's erratic behavior and failure to fulfill his duties, in addition to accusations that he had gone insane. However, according the US Constitution, the only offences for which judges could be forcibly removed were high crimes or misdemeanors. Although Pickering was an unstable and disagreeable person, his behavior did not warrant impeachment under the law.

Jefferson, however, decided Pickering's time in office had come to an end. On February 4, 1803, he passed evidence of Pickering's drunkenness and unlawful rulings to the US House of Representatives, who voted to impeach Pickering on March 2, 1803. The Federalists were scandalized. Accusations that Democratic-Republicans were trying to dominate the judicial system by removing judges from office polarized Washington.

DANGEROUS DESIRE

Jefferson's political choices were not the only objectionable parts of his life. Accounts persist to this day of Jefferson taking Sally Hemings, one of the 600 slaves he owned, as a concubine. Hemings was 14 years old when she traveled with Jefferson's daughter Maria to Paris in 1787. There, she met the recently widowed 44-year-old future president who was serving as the United States Ambassador to France.

> **Thomas Jefferson** was also an architect who designed his own home (Monticello) as well as the University of Virginia's rotunda and the Virginia State Capitol at Richmond. Monticello and the University of Virginia are both on the World Heritage list. Jefferson referred to architecture as "the hobby of my old age."

Hemings—Jefferson's wife's half-sister (Martha Wayles Skelton, Jefferson's wife, passed away in 1782)—was a nursemaid and companion to Jefferson's daughter Maria, and a lady's maid, a chambermaid, and seamstress to his daughter Martha.

According to Madison Hemings' (Sally's son) memoir, Jefferson impregnated Hemings in Paris. Although slavery in France had been abolished in 1789, Jefferson forced Hemings to return to the United States with him. Their first child died soon after their return from Paris, but Jefferson's personal records note that he was the father of her six children who were conceived between 1795 and 1808. He promised to free all of the children he fathered with Hemings when they reached 21 years of age.

In 1802 journalist James T. Callender—after being denied the position of Postmaster of Richmond, Virginia—published allegations that Jefferson had taken Hemings as his personal concubine and fathered several of her children. Jefferson never publicly denied the accusation.

Jefferson freed five slaves with the last name Hemings in his will. He also petitioned the state legislature for each of them to remain in Virginia. However, Jefferson did not free Sally Hemings. He kept her enslaved as part of his estate and recorded her "value" as fifty dollars.

FACT OR FICTION

The historical debate continues regarding whether or not Jefferson actually fathered children with Hemings. Many scholars and biographers now agree that there is enough evidence to prove that it is true.

In 1998, a panel of researchers conducted a DNA test of the Hemings' DNA and confirmed that there was a match with the Jefferson's ancestry. In an interview with PBS, Annette Gordon-Reed, author of *Thomas Jefferson and Sally Hemings: An American Controversy*, said of the affair, "It's tremendously important for people . . . as a way of inclusion. Nathan Huggins [an African-American historian, author, and educator] said that the Sally Hemings story was a way of establishing black people's birthright to America."

In many ways, Thomas Jefferson conforms to the saying, "The bigger the name the deeper the dirt." An immensely talented thinker, and yet a politician not above pettiness, Jefferson lived a personal life full of compromise and complexity. That Hemings was his 14-year-old slave, half-sister-in-law, and likely mother of six unacknowledged, also slave, children, speaks to the intricacies of early American life. By comparison, later presidents' controversies can seem banal.

FAMILY SECRETS

EVEN AFTER DEATH, JEFFERSON SHOCKS THE NATION

Still image from *Jefferson in Paris*, a 1995 feature-length film exploring Jefferson's relationship with Sally Hemings against the backdrop of the French Revolution.

Madison Hemings, son of Sally Hemings, Jefferson's slave and taken mistress, first claimed a connection to Thomas Jefferson in an interview with an Ohio newspaper in 1873, titled "Life Among the Lowly, No.1." In it, Madison says of his mother's stay in France:

During that time my mother became Mr. Jefferson's concubine, and when he was called back home she was enceinte by him. He desired to bring my mother back to Virginia with him but she demurred. She was just beginning to understand the French language well, and in France she was free, while if she returned to Virginia she would be re-enslaved. . . . To induce her to do so he promised her extraordinary privileges, and made a solemn pledge that her children should be freed at the age of twenty-one years. . . . She gave birth to four . . . and Jefferson was the father of all of them. . . . We all became free agreeably to the treaty entered by our parents before we were born. We all married and have raised families.

OTHER MEN'S WIVES

PRESIDENT JACKSON SHAKES THE SOCIAL SCENE

For all the glory Jackson gained in the battlefield, and for all the ferocity of his will, his most memorable controversies lie much closer to home—with the complication of his (illegal) marriage. Voted in as the seventh President of the United States after the "Corrupt Bargain" cost him the election of 1824, Andrew Jackson's presidency is considered a turning point in American politics. For the first time since the inception of the Presidential office, the political power of the Commander in Chief passed from established American elites to ordinary voters and political parties. "The Age of Jackson" is considered a return to the Republican values exemplified by Thomas Jefferson, who advocated for limited government and high moral values.

Jackson distinguished himself early as a courier during the American Revolutionary War, and at the age of 13, was captured by the British along with his brother, Robert. Both Jackson brothers nearly starved to death in captivity and

Left: A political cartoon depicts President Andrew Jackson sitting stunned as his Cabinet members, represented as rats, run to escape his falling house.

both contracted smallpox, which killed Robert before their release. Andrew Jackson's mother, Elizabeth Jackson, died from cholera after volunteering to nurse prisoners of war on board ships in the Charleston harbor. In 1781, at the age of 14, Andrew Jackson became an orphan. He blamed the British for the death of his mother and brother and would exact his revenge against them as an army general later in life.

AN IMPERFECT UNION

Jackson became a country lawyer in the frontier territory of Tennessee, eventually rising to the position of Solicitor and then US Representative for Tennessee.

When Jackson first migrated to Nashville in 1788 as Solicitor of the Western District he boarded with Rachel Stockley Donelson, the mother of Rachel Donelson Robards. Rachel had fled from an abusive marriage to Captain Lewis Robards, of Harrodsburg, Kentucky, after he reportedly beat her. Rachel, a great beauty, was described as having "lustrous black eyes, dark glossy hair, full red lips, brunette complexion, though of a brilliant coloring, [and] a sweet oval face rippling with smiles and dimples." When she met a young Andrew Jackson they quickly fell in love.

A friend of Robards heard of the affair and planted a fake article in his own newspaper, saying that the divorce of Robards and Rachel had been finalized, which led Jackson to believe he could marry her freely. After taking their vows in Natchez, Mississippi, in 1791, they soon learned that Lewis Robards had never obtained a divorce from their previous marriage. The marriage between Jackson and Rachel was entirely illegal.

Robards did eventually pursue a divorce on the grounds of Rachel's adultery, and the Jacksons remarried, legally, in 1794. However, the manufactured scandal followed them almost everywhere they went.

GENERAL JACKSON

Jackson's military career set him up for his political one. He defeated the Red Sticks, a group of unified Native American tribes that fought against the White settlers in Tennessee. Jackson earned the nickname "Old Hickory" at the Battle of New Orleans, where he led a little under 5,000 US soldiers to a decisive victory over more than 7,000 British soldiers. His ruthlessness in battle earned him the nickname "Sharp Knife" from the Seminole tribes during the first Seminole War of 1817, as word spread throughout Florida of his executions of British troops in the territory.

As a retired military hero, Andrew Jackson ran for president against John Quincy Adams in 1828. It did not take long for Jackson's and Rachel's marriage to become an issue. Supporters of Adams called Rachel Jackson a "bigamist" for being married to two men at the same time, and an

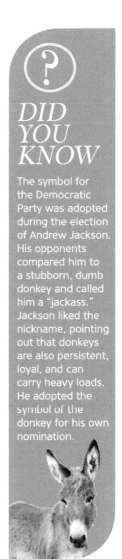

DID YOU KNOW

The symbol for the Democratic Party was adopted during the election of Andrew Jackson. His opponents compared him to a stubborn, dumb donkey and called him a "jackass." Jackson liked the nickname, pointing out that donkeys are also persistent, loyal, and can carry heavy loads. He adopted the symbol of the donkey for his own nomination.

MONEY

Samuel Swartwout was the Collector of Customs under President Jackson. He embezzled $1,225,705.69 and fled to England after his actions were exposed by President Martin Van Buren.

adulteress for flirting with both men while being married. The smear campaign soon went national.

One Cincinnati editor insinuated that Rachel was not the kind of person who should even be allowed on the White House grounds, asking the readership, "Ought a convicted adulteress and her paramour husband be placed in the highest offices of this free and Christian land?" Jackson was infuriated and went so far as to write newspapers guidelines on how to counter the attacks. This proved to be too little too late for Rachel Jackson, who was mortified by the widespread dissemination of her personal life.

The attacks in the press created enormous shame for her, and she spent much of the campaign depressed and crying, which strained a heart condition that had been diagnosed just a few years earlier. She died on December 22, 1828, three days after suffering a heart attack, before ever assuming the role as First Lady.

On December 24, 1828, the day of her funeral, church bells all over Nashville tolled during the hour of her burial and 10,000 Jackson supporters—white and black, wealthy and poor—gathered in crowds at the Hermitage Plantations garden, where the Governor of Tennessee,

President Andrew Jackson (1767–1845) and his Cabinet succumb to the charms of "Celeste," a dainty figure representing Peggy O'Neil, the wife of War Secretary John Eaton.

Sam Houston, served as a pallbearer. "May God Almighty forgive her murderers," Jackson swore at her funeral, blaming Adams and his campaigners for her death. "I never can."

A TALE OF TWO JOHNS

Jackson's personal struggle with Washington's high society proved to be a major factor in "the petticoat affair," one of the biggest scandals during his presidency.

Margaret "Peggy" Eaton was born Margaret O'Neill, the daughter of William O'Neill, who owned The Franklin House, a popular boarding house and bar in Washington. Known for her vivacious character, beauty, and wit, she is quoted as saying she "had the attention of men, young and old, enough to turn a girl's head."

At 17 Margaret married her first husband, John B. Timberlake, a purser in the United States Navy. The couple became

BETTER HALF

Rachel Jackson is said to have calmed the fiery Andrew Jackson. She was able to shut down his impulse to respond to an insult or political remark with a small gesture or soft word. The amount to which Rachel helped him move past his temper was evident during his campaign.

friends with Senator John Henry Eaton, a 28-year old widower, who frequented the Franklin House. The senator helped pay off Timberlake's debts accrued as a result of his alcoholism. He also secured a position for Timberlake in the Navy's Mediterranean Squadron.

While John Timberlake was at sea, Margaret and John Eaton were seen vacationing together and were recorded in hotel logs as man and wife. Rumors abounded. Timberlake died at sea of pulmonary disease and Washington high society speculated that Timberlake had committed suicide after hearing of his wife's affair with the family friend.

Eaton soon sought the advice of his longtime friend, Andrew Jackson, concerning the newly widowed Mrs. Timberlake. Jackson empathized with Eaton and supported their decision to marry, come what may from Washington society.

"If you love Margaret Timberlake go and marry her at once," he is quoted as saying to Eaton, "and shut their mouths." The two were married on New Year's Day, 1829, less than a year after John Timberlake's death.

Jackson and Eaton's relationship was not socially acceptable in Washington society at the time, where rituals of mourning were expected from widows in order to give an acceptable show of respect for their deceased husbands. The wedding resulted in a schism in the Washington social scene. The rift went all the way to the White House, where the Second Lady Floride Calhoun, wife of Vice President John C. Calhoun, led an anti-Peggy group of Cabinet wives in refusing to receive either Eaton or his wife.

Jackson, in an effort to highlight his support for the couple, promoted Eaton as his Secretary of War. While the appointment may have been good for his friend's professional life, it only intensified the scandal. Many of Jackson's own Cabinet questioned Eaton's suitability, including US Army Paymaster, Nathaniel Towson.

Infuriated by the insinuation that social reputation could influence political power, especially after his own personal battle with the whims of high society's judgment, Jackson countered, "Do you suppose that I have been sent here by the people to consult the ladies of Washington as to the proper persons to compose my Cabinet?" Martin Van Buren, the Secretary of State, realized the Democratic Party was being affected by the scandal and took steps to stop the fallout. He successfully convinced Eaton to resign from his post as Secretary of War and then resigned from his own position. Shortly after, every single member of the President's Cabinet followed suit, with the exception of General William T. Barry.

Jackson is said to have stated, "To the next Cabinet may they all be bachelors, or leave their wives at home!"

BASE BARGAINS

DEMOCRACY IMPERILED

1824: CORRUPTION ABOUNDS

The presidential election of 1824 is the only one to have been decided by the House of Representatives, in accordance with the passage of the Twelfth Amendment. Although he received the most electoral votes, the House did not elect Andrew Jackson as president in 1824. Henry Clay—House of Representatives speaker, later to be selected as Secretary of State after helping John Quincy Adams gain the presidency—decided the election.

1876: A DOUBLE VICTORY

The presidential election of 1876 is one of the most contentious and controversial elections in American history. Samuel J. Tilden of New York outpolled Rutherford B. Hayes of Ohio in the popular vote by more than 200,000 ballots; yet, twenty electoral votes were disputed in Florida, Louisiana, South Carolina, and Oregon. The election of 1876 was the first time in 20 years that a Democratic candidate won a majority of the popular vote and did not gain the presidency. The Compromise of 1877 awarded all 20 disputed electoral votes to Hayes, in return for a withdrawal of federal troops from the South.

THE WHITE HOUSE DANDY

QUESTIONS ABOUT BUCHANAN REMAIN

The 15th President of the United States of America inherited a country riven by political and ideological differences over slavery. Though an accomplished politician—he served as congressman, senator, minister to Russia, Secretary of State, and was even offered a position on the supreme court—James Buchanan (above, in a stereoscopic photograph) has consistently been ranked one of the worst presidents of all time because of his failure to stop Southern secession and the beginnings of the Civil War.

He was no better in his personal life. Prior to taking office, Buchanan was engaged to marry a 15 year-old girl named Ann Caroline Coleman. However, she broke off the engagement and mysteriously passed away shortly after. Later in life, Buchanan would be dogged by whispers of homosexuality concerning his relationship with William Rufus King. Buchanan, it seems, was a man on whom fate alternately smiled and turned her back.

EARLY SUCCESS, AND TRAGEDY

Buchanan's political career started early, when, after being admitted to the bar in 1812, he won a seat to the Pennsylvania House of Representatives at the age of 23. He served in legislation from 1814 until 1819, and fell in love with Ann Caroline Coleman, the daughter of a rich merchant in the iron trade. Both Buchanan's family and the Coleman's opposed the match. Some claimed that Buchanan was only interested in her money; others stated the 15-year-old Coleman was much too young.

High society in Pennsylvania was scandalized after the announcement of the engagement between Buchanan and Coleman and the rumor mill around the couple flourished. Gossip soon spread that Buchanan was seeing another woman. When the accusations reached the young Ann's ears, she called off the engagement and died a few days later. The visiting doctor. reported her death as "hysteria" but privately believed she had overdosed on laudanum. The Coleman family was devastated at the loss, blamed Buchanan for her death, and barred him from the funeral. Buchanan, traumatized from the experience, vowed never to marry again. This promise, however, did not stop him from pursuing other intimate prospects.

NEW ROMANCE

In grief, Buchanan dedicated himself to his work. He overcame public resentment over the death of his young fiancé, and managed to win a seat to the US House of Representatives in 1820.

In Washington he lived with William Rufus King, sharing boardinghouse rooms and a distinct taste for clothing, food, and public appearance. King referred to their relationship as a "communion," and they were dubbed the "Siamese twins" by those in Washington, who remarked on their closeness and likeness in character.

Both are described as effeminate, romantic, fussy, having eccentric taste in fashion, and taking meticulous care of their appearance. They attended social functions together, and Andrew Jackson, a mentor for the young Buchanan, dubbed them "Miss Nancy" and "Aunt Fancy," while Aaron V. Brown, a contemporary of Buchanan's, referred to King as Buchanan's "better half."

Buchanan planned to run with King as president and vice president in 1844, though Buchanan instead served as secretary of state under President James K. Polk. King was appointed United States Minister to France. Buchanan wrote "I am now 'solitary and alone,' having no companion in the house with me. I have gone wooing several gentlemen, but have not succeeded with any one of them."

[
Under Buchanan's watch, seven states left the Union. Buchanan was considered the consummate lame duck president and a compulsory equivocator.
]

DID YOU KNOW

Daniel Sickles was the first person to ever successfully use the temporary insanity legal defense in order to justify the murder of Philip Barton Key II, who was having an affair with Sickles' wife. While awaiting trial in jail, Sickles received a supportive personal note from President James Buchanan, with whom he had worked in London.

Rumors of King and Buchanan's relationship have persisted since those heady days in the 1830s and 40s. The letter describing Buchanan's loneliness after King's departure is printed in *Men Like That: A Southern Queer History*, where Buchanan is celebrated as the nation's first gay president. King died of tuberculosis in 1853, three years before Buchanan would be elected president of the United States. Buchanan described him as "among the best, the purest and most consistent public men I have known."

THE BACHELOR PRESIDENT

As the US president in the years leading up to the Civil War, Buchanan was unable to temper the disputes between politicians regarding slavery's legality in the United States of America.

The tension in Washington boiled over under Buchanan's watch when Preston Brooks (a Democrat) beat Senator Charles Sumner (a Massachusetts abolitionist) with a cane on the floor of the United States Senate on May 22, 1856.

Days earlier, Sumner made a speech denouncing those who advocated for the new territory of Kansas to be made a slave-holding state. In his speech, Sumner compared Senator Butler, Brooks' distant cousin, with Don Quixote, saying Butler had embraced slavery as his own harlot. "Of course he has chosen a mistress to whom he has made his vows," said Sumner of Butler, "who, though ugly to others, is always lovely to him."

Left: Portrait of President Buchanan (1791-1868), the 15th president. He held office from 1857-1861.

Brooks was enraged and confronted Sumner, beating him over the head with his cane until it broke. Sumner staggered up the aisle of the Senate floor until he collapsed, unconscious. It was three years before Sumner could return to the Senate. The head trauma caused him chronic pain until the end of his life.

Brooks was given a $300 fine and a motion was issued to expel him from the House. The motion failed, but Brooks resigned his seat soon after. In the North, legislators and citizens alike were horrified by his actions. In the South, Brooks' party and constituents celebrated his attack as a legitimate act upholding the honor of his family and the South. Many supporters even mailed him replacement canes. Soon after, he was reelected to his House seat. This outraged citizens of the North. Many House members viewed Brooks' outburst as an example of Southern brutality associated with slavery. The growing hostility between the North and South, of course, contributed to the start of the American Civil War, which began less than five years later.

A DIS-ORIENTING DEMISE

ZACHARY TAYLOR AND THE SHORTEST TERM SERVED

Zachary Taylor served only 16 months of his presidential term before his demise and is considered one of the least influential presidents of all time—he had no real interest in politics, but was convinced to lead the Whig Party ticket because of his success in the Mexican-American war. During Taylor's time in office, despite being a slaveholder himself, he avoided the question of expanding slavery (hoping to preserve the Union) and shifted his attention to statehood for New Mexico and California. Unfortunately, Taylor fell severely ill after attending holiday celebrations at the Washington Monument in July of 1850. Fever, headaches, diarrhea, and extreme thirst followed as Taylor's chances of recovery diminished. His last words were published in newspapers around the country:

> *I should not be surprised if this were to terminate in my death. I did not expect to encounter what has beset me since my elevation to the Presidency. God knows I have endeavored to fulfill what I conceived to be an honest duty. But I have been mistaken. My motives have been misconstrued, and my feelings most grossly outraged.*

GRANT

A SOLDIER DOES NOT A STATESMAN MAKE

Ulysses S. Grant's two terms in office (1869–1877) are widely regarded as some of the most corrupt to ever take place in the presidential office. His popularity as a hero in the American Civil War slipped as scandals and outcry against the corruption of his office damaged his reputation.

What originally looked to be a promising administration, built on the work of his predecessor Andrew Jackson, turned into utter disaster and ended with the nation heading into a severe economic depression.

Above: A scene from the Mexican-American War, the *Battle of Buena Vista*.

ONLY IN AMERICA

The son of an orphan who built a successful life for himself as a tanner, Grant graduated from the United States Military Academy at West Point in 1843 and served in the Mexican-American War in 1846. He led a cavalry charge at the Battle of Resaca de la Palma and volunteered to dispatch messages through sniper-lined streets on horseback. By the end of the war, he had been promoted to temporary captain and earned a reputation as a gentlemanly horse soldier.

Grant was promoted to permanent captain in the summer of 1853 and assigned to command troops at Fort Humboldt in California. Soon rumors about his drinking habits and penchant for off-duty intoxication spread up the ranks. (Grant's grandfather, Noah, came from a prominent New England family but ruined his fortune, family, and reputation through drink.) Grant was asked to resign his position in 1854 as reports of his intemperance grew.

The next seven years were lean for the young Grant, who had no civilian vocation and little luck at the trades he pursued: farming, leather tanning, and selling firewood. It wasn't until the American Civil War began in 1861 that Grant was called back to serve in the military. He quickly rose through the ranks of the Union Army and reestablished his reputation as a soldier able to succeed in an army consisting of mostly untrained and unskilled volunteers.

THE LEGEND EMERGES

Grant was promoted to colonel of the Union Army in June of 1861 and led his troops against a Confederate attack at

Fort Henry on the Tennessee River. The fort was strategically important to the Union and its control would allow gunboats to control supply lines for hundreds of miles in either direction. Following the victory, Lincoln promoted Grant to major general. The press celebrated him as a hero; up to that point Union military accomplishments had been few and far between. It was at Fort Henry that he earned the nickname, "Unconditional Surrender Grant," for his refusal to accept terms from the Confederate commander, Brigadier General Lloyd Tilghman.

His many successes in battles during the war caused Grant's star to rise, both in the Army through successful promotion to lieutenant general of all Union armies, and in the press where speculation of an early Union victory over the Confederate forces sparked talks of his candidacy for presidency.

However, an early victory was not accomplished. It took nearly four years and more than 350,000 casualties before Grant accepted Robert E. Lee's surrender at Appomattox Court House on April 9, 1865. Five days later Lincoln was fatally shot by John Wilkes Booth at Ford's Theater and died the next morning.

By the end of the war, Grant was a national hero and was chosen as the presidential candidate for the Republican Party in the election of 1868. In his letter of acceptance, Grant concluded with "Let us have peace," which became his campaign slogan.

AN EARNEST ENDEAVOR

Grant won the election in a landslide, receiving three times as many Electoral College votes as his rival for the presidency,

Left: City Point, Virginia, was the hub of the Union Army and served as General Ulysses S. Grant's headquarters. Grant's son and wife were with him at City Point when this photo was taken in 1864.

Horatio Seymour. The 46-year-old Grant was the youngest president ever elected at the time.

Facing the new President was the task of reconstructing a country destroyed by warfare and integrating the recalcitrant Southern states back into the Union—albeit on the North's terms. In his inaugural address Grant urged the ratification of the Fifteenth Amendment, which would give Black Americans the right to vote, and said he would approach Reconstruction without sectional pride.

Grant advocated for systemic federal enforcement of civil rights in the South and relied on his army, as well as the Justice Department, to implement his vision. The United States issued a large amount of public debt in order to finance the reconstruction of the South; this included the introduction of paper dollars, not backed by gold, into the marketplace. It was generally believed that the United States would eventually redeem the money for gold. Speculators, seeing an opportunity for private profit at public expense, set the stage for Grant's first policy scandal.

THE CARPETBAGGERS

In the summer of 1869 a group of financiers headed by Jay Gould sought to profit off the paper currency by buying large amounts of gold. They recruited Grant's brother-in-law, Abel Corbin, into their scheme, and through him gained influence on Grant. Gould and his partner Jim Fisk took every opportunity to convince President Grant not to buy back the paper money for gold, keeping the market in their favor.

Grant never supported Gould's scheme but his plans to sell government gold in order to buy back money was delayed long enough to make the speculators a handsome profit. When Grant was alerted to what was happening he impulsively ordered the sale of $4 million in government gold and inadvertently caused its price to plummet.

Many investors, who had taken out loans to buy gold, were ruined. The day became known as Black Friday. Gould, however, had gotten wind of Grant's decision to sell and escaped financial harm.

A congressional hearing was held and an article appeared in 1870 titled The New York Gold Conspiracy. Grant was attacked over allegations that he had participated in the corruption and the nickname "the Era of Good Stealing" was given to his presidential tenure.

Unfortunately, this was only the first of many incidences of corruption during Grant's presidency.

The day before Grant's second inauguration Congress passed what is popularly known as the Salary Grab Act, which doubled the salary of the president and supreme court justices. Also hidden in the language of the Act was a retroactive 50 percent pay increase for the members of Congress.

The nation was facing a severe economic downturn after the Panic of

DID YOU KNOW

Prior to being appointed as Grant's private secretary (today's chief of staff), Orville Elias Babcock served in the Union army as Grant's aide-de-camp and participated in Grant's Overland Campaign in 1864. Having earned Grant's loyalty, Babcock was defended by Grant in an infamous 1876 deposition earning his acquittal.

1873, a financial crisis that grew from speculation in railroad bonds and caused a major depression that lasted through 1879. Factories across the country laid off workers, and 55 of the nation's railroads failed. The public was appalled at the apparent greed of Washington politicians who sought to increase their salaries as the nation fell into misery.

Just two years later, in 1875, the Whiskey Ring scandal was exposed in the press, cementing Grant's reputation as one of the most corrupt presidents of all time. The scheme involved a complex conspiracy of government agents, politicians, and whiskey distillers and distributors who funneled over $3 million (More than $57 million, adjusted for inflation) of federal tax revenues into the pockets of mostly Republican politicians. The ring had been operating for years, and historians have speculated that money from the scheme was used to elect Grant.

Attorney James Broadhead, who had been appointed by Grant to lead the trials against the conspirators, indicted President Grant's own private secretary, Orville E. Babcock, as a member of the ring. Before the investigation was finished, more than

110 convictions were made and the reputation of the Republican Party was in tatters.

While never directly connected with the scheme, President Grant became emblematic of the corruption that took place in his office. By the end of his presidency Southern disenchantment had grown so strong that the political parties made an informal agreement to largely abandon Reconstruction. Known as the Compromise of 1877, the federal government pulled its troops out of the southern states in return for accepting the election of Rutherford B. Hayes, a Republican, as president.

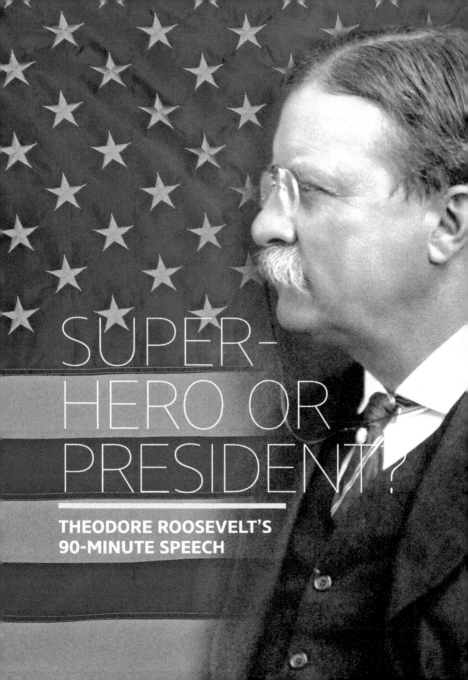

SUPER-HERO OR PRESIDENT?

THEODORE ROOSEVELT'S 90-MINUTE SPEECH

Theodore Roosevelt performed his duties with an energy that could power a large American city. For example, Roosevelt was shot in the chest while campaigning in Wisconsin. He declined treatment and gave a 90-minute speech with blood oozing down his shirt. "Ladies and Gentlemen, I don't know whether you fully understand that I have just been shot," Roosevelt announced. "But it takes more than that to kill a Bull Moose."

A statesman, scholar, author, police commissioner, sheriff, soldier, rancher, progressive reformer and much more, Roosevelt's accomplishments in the White House are unmatched more than 100 years after leaving office. An unforgiving moralist that embodied the colloquialism, "Walk the walk," he scandalized the Republican Party by washing away its dirt. Roosevelt possessed an impatience with his political peers that compelled him to run for president two more times after he'd already served two terms.

HARDING AND THE OHIO GANG

THE COST OF KEEPING QUESTIONABLE COMPANY

The Republicans faced a serious problem in the 1920 campaign. The party was split between progressive followers of the late Theodore Roosevelt and conservatives who opposed them and lacked strong leadership. Their candidates reflected the internal discord with four different contenders running for the position. The eventual winner, Warren G. Harding, was initially the least popular of the group.

Republican senators were divided and so held a meeting at the Blackstone Hotel in Chicago to discuss the nomination. After a nightlong presidential horse-trading session, Harding was chosen as the best possible compromise candidate, thanks in part to the support of his friend Harry Daugherty (who would later become his campaign manager).

The setting for Harding's nomination would echo throughout his presidency: friends secretly cutting deals in his name without his knowledge.

Above: Harry M. Daugherty (1860-1941), testifying at the Senate Investigation of the Teapot Dome scandal.

FRONT PORCH CAMPAIGNING

Harding made his fortune as a newspaperman in Ohio. His broadsheet, the *Marion Daily Star*, was the most popular newspaper in city, and he used his knowledge of the media to his advantage. His campaign was the first to use modern advertising techniques, employing telemarketers and speakers, and enlisting celebrities such as Thomas Edison and Henry Ford.

His platform promised a "Return to Normalcy" following the end of World War I.

> *There isn't anything the matter with world civilization, except that humanity is viewing it through a vision impaired in a cataclysmal war,"* said Harding in a speech leading up to election "America's present need is not heroics, but healing; not nostrums, but normalcy; not revolution, but restoration," he affirmed. "My best judgment of America's needs is to steady down, to get squarely on our feet, to make sure of the right path. . . . Let us stop to consider that tranquility at home is more precious than peace abroad, and that both our good fortune and our eminence are dependent on the normal forward stride of all the American people.*

Harding won the election in a landslide, receiving 60 percent of the popular vote, and Harding enjoyed great popularity, both nationally and internationally for the first 28 months of his presidency. The administration cut taxes and federal spending and reduced unemployment by 10 percent. On the international front he pursued peace with Germany, Japan, and Central America.

For all intents and purposes, Harding was making good on his promise to focus on stabilizing the American psyche after the damage done by years of war. However, trouble brewed in the backrooms of the White House, fueled by the questionable

TEAPOT DOME

The Teapot Dome is one of the most notorious scandals of the Harding administration. Secretary of the Interior Albert Bacon Fall sold exclusive rights to the Teapot Dome (an oil reserve in Wyoming) to Harry Sinclair of the Mammoth Oil Company.

appointments Harding made to his Cabinet and in key positions of the administration. His reputation suffered for it.

LOW FRIENDS IN HIGH PLACES

Harding appointed Harry Daugherty, his campaign manager and long time supporter, to the post of US Attorney General. Daugherty quickly gained a reputation for corruption and graft. A congressional investigation into the Justice Department in 1923 ended without any charges, but many believed Daugherty was a serious liability for Harding.

Another of Harding's problematic appointments was Charles Forbes as the first Director of the Veterans' Bureau. Described as a "dashing playboy" in Washington, the two became friends after meeting on vacation in Hawaii. As director, Forbes is known for ignoring the needs of wounded veterans, embezzling approximately $2 million ($27 million adjusted for inflation) from monies intended to build veterans' hospitals, and retaining kickbacks and personal gifts from building contractors. His accomplice was Charles F. Cramer, general counsel of the Veterans' Bureau.

Portrait of President Warren Harding (1865–1923), the twenty-ninth President of the United States from 1921–1923.

Furious at the accusations coming out of the Bureau, Harding summoned Forbes to the White House and grabbed him by the throat "as a dog would a rat" calling him a "double-crossing bastard." Harding forced Forbes to resign his position and Forbes fled to Europe, leaving the newly created Veterans' Bureau in shambles.

The scandal, however, was far from over. After Forbes' resignation in 1923, scrutiny on the Bureau intensified. Cramer could not handle the pressure and killed himself only one month later. Cramer wasn't the only member of Harding's "Ohio Gang," the nickname given to the president's imported circle of friends, to take his own life amidst scandal.

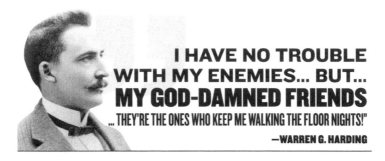

I HAVE NO TROUBLE WITH MY ENEMIES... BUT... MY GOD-DAMNED FRIENDS ... THEY'RE THE ONES WHO KEEP ME WALKING THE FLOOR NIGHTS!"
—WARREN G. HARDING

Ten weeks after the discovery of Cramer's body, Jesse W. Smith, Attorney General Daugherty's aide, was found at Daugherty's apartment with a gunshot wound to the head. His death was ruled a suicide, but as the investigation unfolded, it became clear that Smith had cheated various conspirators out of tens of millions of dollars.

Smith had used his proximity to the administration to cultivate some perks of his own, including the selling of liquor licenses, granting of parole, and the arrangement of other contracts. The day before Smith died, Harding had a long and emotional argument with him at the White House. Although the exact content of the meeting is unknown, it is presumed Harding confronted Smith on his corruption and illegal activities. Alabama Senator James Thomas Heflin said on the floor of the Senate, "Nobody else knew what he [Smith] knew and with him dead there's nobody to tell the story—so Jesse Smith was murdered."

HARD WORK NEVER DONE

Harding found the presidency increasingly difficult to manage. The usually buoyant and magnetic Ohioan looked increasingly solemn and frail. He told the National Press Club that he could "never find himself done." He explained, "I don't believe there is a human being who can do all the work there is to be done in the president's office. It seems as though I have been president for twenty years." His health in decline and his spirits dashed, Harding embarked on a trip to Alaska in the summer of 1923 to resolve bureaucratic conflicts in the territory and to remove himself from the stress of his office.

Herbert Hoover, who served as Secretary of Commerce under Harding, joined him on the expedition and recalled the president ruminating over the growing scandals in his administration. Harding asked Hoover what he would do if he knew a scandal was brewing, to which Hoover replied, "Publish it, and at least get credit for integrity on your side."

The strain of dealing with the mishaps of his Cabinet and staff weighed heavily on Harding. He became morose and noticeably strained as he returned from the trip. As his train approached San Francisco he complained of pains in his upper abdominal region, and his doctors confirmed that he had suffered a cardiac episode.

While resting in the Palace Hotel he suffered an acute coronary artery occlusion while his wife read to him from the Saturday Evening Post. He died instantly.

GETTING PERSONAL WITH PERSONNEL

NAVY INVESTIGATIONS
IN NEWPORT NEWS

The United States Navy decided to investigate the illicit sexual behavior of Navy personnel in Newport, Rhode Island in 1919. Navy officers Thomas Brunelle and Ervin Arnold gave detailed reports of effeminate behavior, cross-dressing, sexual activity, drinking liquor, and cocaine use. After reading the reports from Navy officers, a court concluded that a thorough investigation was warranted. Franklin Roosevelt, then a 37-year-old Assistant Secretary of the Navy, approved the investigation into the homosexual subculture in Newport. Chief Machinist Mate Ervin Arnold, also a former Connecticut state detective, undertook the investigation and decided an infiltration approach was best.

Choosing his investigators based on their youth and looks, thirteen agents submitted daily candid descriptions of homosexual acts to Arnold. Arrests began on April 4, 1919; a total of 17 sailors were charged with sodomy and scandalous conduct. Most were sent to a naval prison; two were dishonorably discharged, and two more were found innocent.

Later, a subcommittee of the Senate Committee on Naval Affairs denounced Roosevelt for the methods used in the investigation. *The New York Times* reported that while most of the evidence was unprintable the committee believed Roosevelt knew that "enlisted men of the navy were used as participants in immoral practices for the purpose of obtaining evidence."

LUST AND MARRIAGE

SERVING AS
PHILANDERER-IN-CHIEF

When Dan Rather sat down with former President Bill Clinton for an interview in 2004, three years after the end of his term, the central question was "why?" Why had Clinton, who led an exemplary career as President of the United States from 1993 to 2001 engaged in an affair with a White House aide that almost cost him the Presidency? His answer, and probably that of many other powerful men, was direct: "Because I could." Philandering in the halls of power is as old as power itself and many presidents have enjoyed a paramour in the White House. Here's a list of some of the most famous White House indiscretions.

THOMAS JEFFERSON

While Jefferson was publicly against the institution of slavery, calling it an "abominable crime," he owned over 600 slaves in his lifetime, one of whom was a 14-year-old Sally Hemings, a nurse to his daughter and mother of six of Jefferson's children.

During his Presidency, a disgruntled political journalist, James T. Callender, reported on the situation in 1802, saying of Jefferson, "it is well known that the man, whom it delighteth the people to honor, and for many years past has kept, as his concubine, one of his own slaves." Jefferson never denied the accusation.

WARREN HARDING

President Warren Harding served the country for only three years before dying of heart disease in San Francisco on August 2, 1923.

Left: Marilyn Monroe sings "Happy Birthday, Mr. President" at one of her last major public appearances before her death.

Above: Florence Harding, showing marked signs of improving from her illness, aboard houseboat of the Washington publisher Edward B. McLean at Palm Beach, Florida March 13, 1923.

Rumors circulated in the press after his wife, Florence Harding, refused to allow an autopsy on her husband's body. One former Harding administration member claimed that Florence had poisoned her husband as punishment for his numerous infidelities.

After Harding's death, Nan Britton, a native of Harding's hometown, Marion, Ohio, publicly claimed that the former President was the father of her daughter, born shortly before his election in 1920. In 1928, she published *The President's Daughter*, in which she claims to have had an affair with Harding throughout his presidency.

Another of Harding's famous affairs was with Caroline Phillips, wife of James Phillips, a prominent businessman in Marion, Ohio. She holds the infamous distinction of being the only woman to ever successfully blackmail a major political party; the Republicans sent her to Asia and the Pacific Islands to get her out of the press. She was also promised an annual stipend for the remainder of her life in return for her silence on the Harding affair.

FRANKLIN DELANO ROOSEVELT

Lucy Mercer Rutherfurd—hired as the social secretary of Eleanor Roosevelt in 1914—was an established part of the Roosevelt household, and a good friend to Eleanor. In 1916, while Eleanor and the children were away on vacation, she and FDR began an affair that would last a lifetime.

Lucy was fired by Eleanor and left the Roosevelt household when the affair came to light. But the lovers hardly skipped a beat. Franklin was serving as Assistant Secretary of the Navy, and when Lucy enlisted, she was assigned to his office.

Despite Roosevelt's promise to his wife that he would never see his mistress again and although Mercer was married to Winthrop Rutherfurd, Roosevelt and Mercer continued to see each other over the next three decades. When Roosevelt suffered a fatal cerebral hemorrhage at his "Little White House" in Warm Springs, Georgia, Mercer was there by his side.

DID YOU KNOW

Following Franklin Roosevelt's affair with Lucy Mercer, First Lady Eleanor Roosevelt began focusing her efforts on more public affairs. The First Lady also began openly disagreeing with her husband's political stances while advocating for women's equality and full rights for African Americans, Asian Americans, and World War II refugees.

Eleanor, of course, is known for her own long list of affairs, which include Lorena Hickock, Harry Hopkins, Earl Miller, and David Gurewitsch.

DWIGHT D. EISENHOWER

While most of Eisenhower's biographers deny the affair, rumors persist of a relationship between him and his chauffer, Kay Summersby. Summersby was a former fashion model who joined the British Mechanised Transport Corps during the Second World War in 1939. She was an excellent navigator of London's streets and when the United States joined the Allies in December 1941, she was assigned as a chauffer to Major General Dwight Eisenhower.

In 1975, 30 years after the affair, Summersby published her autobiography, *Past Forgetting: My Love Affair with Dwight D. Eisenhower*. She was explicit about the details of their affair, which are still disputed to this day.

JOHN F. KENNEDY

On May 19, 1962, Marilyn Monroe took the stage at Madison Square Garden wearing a skintight dress and her trademark bright red lipstick. The occasion: the 45th birthday of President John F. Kennedy. More than 15,000 people were in attendance; all witnessed Monroe's sultry, personal rendition of "Happy Birthday, Mr. President." Kennedy's wife, Jacqueline, was not present.

Biographer Robert Dallek described Kennedy as a "compulsive womanizer" and reportedly regularly told Cabinet members,

President John F. Kennedy and first lady Jacqueline Kennedy as they attend one of five inaugural balls in Washington. Jacqueline sports her calling-card hairdo by Kenneth Batelle (also Marilyn Monroe's go to stylist).

administration members, and foreign politicians alike of his need to seduce women.

While in the White House, Kennedy was linked to Marlene Dietrich, Mimi Alford, Judith Campbell Exner, Angie Dickinson, and Ellen Rometesch, though none proved as scandalous as his affair with Marilyn Monroe. Kennedy's birthday celebration was one of the last public performances of Monroe's career; she died several weeks later from an overdose.

LYNDON B. JOHNSON

Johnson's antics in the White House are the stuff of legend. Known for his penchant for exposing his genitals, driving his staff to exhaustion, and publicly humiliating his aides and enemies, his extramarital affairs shocked few and only added to the lore of his many scandalous behaviors while in the Oval Office.

On November 5, 1982, Madeleine Duncan Brown held a news conference at the Dallas Press Club and announced that she had had an extramarital affair with Johnson for almost 20 years. Her claim was published in *People Magazine* and her son filed a $10.5 million paternity suit against Lady Bird Johnson. The suit was dismissed in 1989 after Brown failed to appear in court. In 1990, Brown died from lymphatic cancer.

BILL CLINTON

Clinton's infamous affair with 22-year old White House intern Monica Lewinsky rocked the nation when evidence of the affair broke in 1998. Clinton publicly denied the affair, famously stating, "I did not have sexual relations with that woman, Miss Lewinsky," in a nationally televised White House news conference.

The House voted to impeach Clinton based on allegations of perjury and obstruction of justice, claiming that Clinton had lied about, and tried to cover up, his relationship with Lewinsky. Clinton was famously presented with Lewinsky's dress, which contained his semen, as well as testimony from Lewinsky that he had inserted a cigar tube into her vagina. Under pressure, Clinton finally confessed saying, "I did have a relationship with Miss Lewinsky that was not appropriate."

LIAR, LIAR

LINCOLN AND A RED-HOT STOVE

Republican Senator Simon Cameron was never a man known for his scruples. Seeking advice about Cameron, Lincoln reportedly asked Thaddeus Stevens (above, in a stereoscopic photograph) if he believed Cameron capable of stealing. Stevens reportedly replied jokingly, "I don't think that he would steal a red-hot stove." Lincoln found himself so tickled by the joke that he repeated it to Cameron, who was not quite as amused. When Cameron demanded an apology, Stevens then told Lincoln, "I believe I told you he would not steal a red-hot stove. I will now take that back."

Cameron served as United States Secretary of War for Abraham Lincoln but resigned after one year amidst controversy over corruption and political favoritism.

THE LAP
OF LUXURY

A FUR COAT SMEARS
AN ADMINISTRATION

Dwight "Ike" Eisenhower was a five-star general in the United States Army during World War II, served as the Supreme Commander of the Allied Forces in Europe, and was the last president to have been born in the 19th century.

He entered the 1952 presidential race as a Republican, running on a platform to crusade against "Communism, Korea, and corruption." Perhaps that is why his staff's behavior came under so much scrutiny. Before Eisenhower had even set foot in the Oval Office, critics questioned those that surrounded him, mainly his vice presidential running mate, Richard Nixon.

Nixon was accused of improprieties related to a fund established by his financial backers to reimburse him for the political expenses he incurred while campaigning. The fund was entirely legal, but Nixon was under public scrutiny because of his crusade against graft and corruption in the White House. With his nomination on the line, Nixon took time off from his campaign to fly to Los Angeles and address the American public

Right: Richard Nixon, Republican candidate for the vice presidency, explains an $18,000 expense fund on national television, September 23,1952.

on live television. Scholars rank his speech the sixth most important speech of the 20th century: It marks the beginning of the age of television in American politics.

TRICKY DICK BARES ALL

The half hour of television airtime cost the Republic National Committee $75,000, and was heard by about 60 million Americans, the largest television audience at that time.

In the speech, Nixon explained the purpose of the fund: reimbursements for travel costs, postage for political mailings, and other such expenses related to campaigning. The fund was a necessity, he explained, because he and his family were of modest means and came from a moderate family background. Having spent much of his time in public service, he was not endowed with the personal fortunes of some of his political contemporaries.

His remarks, and especially his open account of his family's finances, touched a chord with many of the millions of viewers, and helped improve public opinion of his and Eisenhower's campaign.

This famous gambit to elicit empathy from viewers gave this speech its famous name: "The Checkers Speech." It echoed a famous speech given by Franklin Roosevelt, eight years to the day before Nixon's—the "Fala Speech." In it, Roosevelt mocked his detractors who accused him of misusing public funds to retrieve his own dog, Fala, after he accidently left the canine in the Aleutian Islands.

{ **Nixon's financial striptease** The strategy of using emotional appeal and cultural identity rather than political rhetoric to gain support. }

FUR AFFAIR

Nixon was able to turn a controversy into a campaign coup, but another member of Eisenhower's administration was not so slick.

Sherman Adams, Eisenhower's Chief of Staff for six years, ended up resigning his position amidst a scandal over a fur coat. Adams was one of the most powerful men in Washington during his time serving Eisenhower; with the exception of Cabinet members and advisors, every request for access to the president had to go through his office.

He earned many nicknames while working in the White House including "The Abominable No-Man" for rejecting access to the president, and "The Boss," from the perceived belief that he had an incredible amount of power in Washington.

In 1958 a House subcommittee revealed that Adams had accepted an expensive vicuña coat from Bernard Goldfine, a Boston textile manufacturer who was under investigation for Federal Trade Commission violations.

Goldfine had violated the Wool Products Labeling Act by producing textiles with more nylon than was advertised on

DID YOU KNOW

The vicuña is a South American camelid that lives in the high alpine areas of the Andes. It is believed to be a wild ancestor of domesticated alpacas and they produce small amounts of very fine wool. This wool is extremely expensive because of its rarity; the animals can only be shorn every three years.

the tag. Adams acquired a full report on the charges Goldfine faced and provided it to the accused. The investigation was dropped a month later.

The House subcommittee found that Adams received the coat from Goldfine, as well as an expensive Oriental rug, a few mats, and was paid about $2,000 for hotel expenses in New England.

Republicans began calling for Adams' resignation, believing the scandal would hurt the party in the 1958 elections. Eisenhower was also pressured to drop him as he had promised he would not tolerate unethical behavior in his administration. Reluctantly, Eisenhower asked Adams to resign.

Adams' outgoing speech was televised. In it, he spoke of a "campaign of vilification" and that efforts to remove him from the White House "[had] been intended to destroy me and in so doing embarrass the administration of the president of the United States." Eisenhower described his decision to ask Adams to resign as "the most hurtful, the hardest, the most heartbreaking decision" of his presidential career.

Arguably, on the spectrum of scandal, the Adams and Nixon controversies are not the worst. However, they illustrate the scrutiny all administrations receive and the willingness of political opponents to make something salacious out of small indiscretions.

POWER PROCEEDINGS

Understanding the Democratic Presidential Impeachment Process

HOUSE OF REPRESENTATIVES

Allegations presented to the Speaker

Speaker refers information to House Committee on Rules

House Committee Examines & Formalizes Procedure

Sends it to the Judiciary Committee

The Judiciary Committee examines the evidence

VOTE:
IMPEACH OR NOT

Renders the Articles of Impeachment and sends to the floor of the House

The House of Representatives debates the Articles →

50%
REPRESENTATIVES **+ 1 =**
MAJORITY

VOTE:
FORMALLY ACCUSE?

The Senate holds a trial

The Senate votes →

2/3
MAJORITY IS REQUIRED TO CONVICT →

THE SENATE'S VERDICT IS FINAL WITH NO RIGHT OF APPEAL

Impeached by the US House of Representatives, but acquitted by the Senate

Andrew Johnson

Bill Clinton

A KNIGHT AMONG KNAVES

JFK'S MURDER SPARKS DECADES OF CONTROVERSY

Rain poured down on the morning of November 22, 1963, in Fort Worth, Texas, when President John F. Kennedy, on a platform set out in front of the Texas Hotel, thanked his supporters for coming to see him off to Dallas. "There are no faint hearts in Fort Worth," he announced, "and I appreciate your being here this morning."

In the fall of 1963, Kennedy was preparing for his upcoming presidential re-election campaign, which was set to take place the following year. He was confident about extending his term another four years, and happy to be out of Washington, back again on the streets of the nation. He stopped first in Texas where a feud among Democratic Party leaders, as well as a vocal group of extremists, created party divisions in a state he needed in order to secure a second term.

Right: John F. Kennedy with Jacqueline and Caroline, at Hyannis Port, August 1959.

JACKIE KENNEDY

Jackie Kennedy's pink suit was one of her husband's favorites, and he asked her to wear it for their motorcade appearance in Dallas, Texas. Hours later, despite being covered in her husband's blood, she refused to take it off, reportedly saying 'No, I'm going to leave these clothes on. I want them to see what they have done.'

DALLAS LOVES YOU

After speaking to the supporters congregated outside his hotel, Kennedy flew to Dallas where he was scheduled to ride through the city in a presidential motorcade. It was a routine campaign dog-and-pony show that was scheduled to end with lunch at the Dallas Trade Mart.

The route, which had been publicized in several newspapers prior to Kennedy's arrival, took him straight through downtown Dallas and right by the Texas School Book Depository. It was planned so supporters and fans could show their support as the President drove by.

Lee Harvey Oswald began working at the Depository only one month before the president's visit. Oswald was an ex-marine who, after living in the Soviet Union for several months to study socialism, returned to the United States a fervent Castro supporter. He came back to Dallas from his home in Irving, Texas, the Friday before JFK's visit, carrying a large brown paper bag. It contained a 6.5 mm Carcano rifle Oswald had purchased earlier that year.

At 12:29 p.m., Nellie Connally, first lady of Texas, turned to President Kennedy and

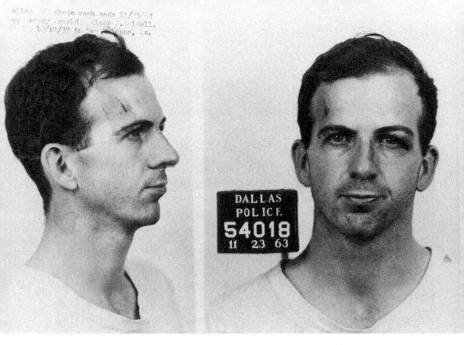

The Dallas Police Department mug shots of Lee Harvey Oswald following his arrest for possible involvement in the John F. Kennedy assassination and the murder of Officer J.D. Tippit.

said, "Mr. President, you can't say Dallas doesn't love you." He responded, "No, you certainly can't." Those were the presidents' last words. At approximately 12:30 p.m., as Kennedy's motorcade drove through Dallas's Dealey Plaza, passing the Depository, Oswald fired three shots from the sixth story corner window at the presidential limousine. Oswald immediately left the building and was on a city bus by 12:40 p.m. After shooting a police officer that approached him, Oswald was captured at the Texas Theatre, just blocks from his home, at 1:40 p.m. By 1:30 a.m. the next morning, Lee Harvey Oswald was arraigned for the murder of Dallas Patrolman J.D. Tippit and the assassination of President John F. Kennedy.

THE AVENGER

Jack Ruby, a nightclub operator, friend of the Mafia, and reported arms smuggler, was devastated by the president's death. Over the next several days he appeared at various locations that would add further layers to the mystery of Kennedy's assassination; the first being Parkland Hospital on November 22, 1963 at 1:30 p.m., where Kennedy was receiving medical care.

He was next spotted in the halls of the Dallas Police Headquarters, on several occasions, as the interrogation and eventual arrest of Lee Harvey Oswald took place behind closed doors.

Newsreel footage from WFAA-TV (Dallas) shows Ruby impersonating a newspaper reporter during a press conference at the Dallas Police Headquarters that night. Witnesses reported

PRESIDENTIAL SCANDALS ON THE BIG SCREEN

1976

REDFORD/HOFFMAN "ALL THE PRESIDENT'S MEN"

JFK Filmmaker Oliver Stone examines the conspiracy surrounding the assassination of President John F. Kennedy.

1995

DEWEY DEFEATS TRUMAN

All The President's Men Directed by Alan J. Pakula, this film is based on Carl Bernstein's and Bob Woodward's investigation of the Watergate scandal.

1991

Truman Based on David McCullough's 1992 historical biography of America's 33rd president, this TV movie depicts Truman's rise to power.

hearing him correct District Attorney Henry Wade on the name of Oswald's pro-Castro organization.

On November 24, Ruby walked into the basement of the Dallas police headquarters and at 11:21 a.m., while police escorted Oswald to an armored car headed for the county jail, stepped out of a crowd of reporters and fired a revolver into Oswald's abdomen.

The American public, who lost a chance at a trial and testimony from Oswald that day, has been trying to find closure on the issue since Kennedy's murder. In 2013, on the 50th anniversary of Kennedy's assassination, polls indicated that 61 percent of Americans believed that Lee Harvey Oswald did not act alone. Citing questionable evidence, unresolved eyewitness testimony, and a possible government cover up, theories abound as to who, or what organization, killed Kennedy.

1998

Primary Colors Directed by Mike Nichols, this 1998 comedy-drama is loosely based on Bill Clinton's 1992 presidential campaign.

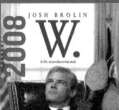

2008

JOSH BROLIN
W.
A life misunderestimated.

W. A biographical drama, also directed by Oliver Stone, that details the life of President George W. Bush.

2012

Lincoln Directed by Steven Spielberg, this epic dramatization focuses on President Abraham Lincoln's effort to abolish slavery.

THE MAGIC BULLET

Several points of the story are still under debate: Oswald and his background, the number of shooters at the scene, and a possible cover-up by the Warren Commission, pieced together by the investigative body after the murder.

Many researchers have pointed out inconsistencies, oversights, exclusion of evidence, and changes made to eyewitness testimony in the Warren Committee investigation.

This theory is supported by former US senator Richard Schweiker, a member of the US Senate Select Committee on Intelligence, who told researcher Anthony Summer, "I believe that the Warren Commission was set up at the time to feed pabulum to the American public for reasons not yet known and that one of the biggest cover-ups in the history of the country occurred at that time." Case in point: The "magic bullet" theory, which asserts that a single bullet ripped through Kennedy's suit coat from behind, punctured the right side of his body, exited his throat below his Adam's apple, pierced Texas Governor John Connally's back, shattered his right rib, exited the front of his chest, shot through his right wrist, and, finally, buried itself in Connally's right thigh.

Unfortunately for conspiracy theorists, this evidence has been widely supported through the years. A NASA scientist who studied the bullet's trajectory for the House Committee on Assassinations found nothing suspect. In 2004 the Discovery Channel re-enacted the shooting and found nothing implausible about the theory, and the American Bar Association commissioned a 3-D computer animation that eventually supported it.

Debate also continues over the number of shots fired at the Kennedy motorcade. Though the official count was three from

Oswald's rifle, others insist there were four. Many maintain that Oswald did not act alone that day and that a second gunman was positioned at a grassy knoll on the north side of Elm Street along the motorcade.

Audiotapes from the shooting have sparked large controversy over their interpretation, speed, and synchronicity. Most experts agree with the official count of three gunshots heard.

UNUSUAL SUSPECTS

Many conspiracy theorists point to the Central Intelligence Agency (CIA) as the organization behind the Kennedy assassination. After the failure of the Bay of Pigs invasion Kennedy was reportedly embittered against the CIA. In a *New York Times* article from 1966, Kennedy is quoted as saying to an official in his administration that he wanted "to splinter the C.I.A. in a thousand pieces and scatter it to the winds."

The same article states "few persons in or out of the American government know much about its work" and that a senator interviewed for the article "proved to know very little about, but to fear very much, its operations."

To complicate matters further, Allen Dulles, the former head of the CIA who was forced to resign during the Kennedy administration, was appointed to the Warren Commission, a clear conflict of interest. There are also those who suspect Oswald was a double agent working both for the CIA and the Soviet Union and was instructed to kill Kennedy.

Sammy Giancana (1908–1975), American mobster and boss of the 'Chicago Outfit,' arriving at the US District Court in Chicago. Giancana was jailed for a year afer refuisng to cooperate with the grand jury investigation.

MAFIA

The Kennedy family had ties to Mafia boss Sam Giancana, former head of the Chicago crime syndicate. Joe Kennedy, John's father, had been involved in the boot-legging business with Giancana during the prohibition era. When his son entered the 1960 West Virginia primary, Joe allegedly asked the mobster for help securing the win.

When Kennedy made it into the White House, he enlisted the help of Giancana, as well as other Mafia leaders, in a plot to kill Fidel Castro. The Cuban leader had made powerful enemies when he closed down the mob's casinos after taking power in 1959.

By 1963 those same mob bosses were angered by the Bay of Pigs fiasco and embittered by Attorney General Robert F. Kennedy's (the President's brother) crusade against high profile crime. They had the motivation, means, and resources, to have Kennedy's term, and life, ended.

KGB

Pointing to Oswald's defection to the Soviet Union in 1959, some believe that he maintained connections with the Kremlin after his return to the United States two years later and was acting as an agent of either Cuban or Soviet Union interests when he shot the president.

Research into Oswald's time in Russia, however, points to a much different relationship with state officials. His life in Russia was heavily monitored and choreographed by the KGB, his friends were corralled by security agents to provide information about his activities, and his apartment was monitored by agents who drilled a peephole through one of its walls.

The spying and monitoring by the KGB eventually drove Oswald from the Soviet Union back to the United States, disillusioned by the socialist state. After the assassination the Soviets communicated to President Johnson that they had not been involved.

PLENTY OF DATA, FEW ANSWERS

Thanks to the JFK Assassination Records Collection Act of 1992, more than six million pages of documentation have been released to the American public. One revelation is that the CIA in fact buried its knowledge of Oswald's activity before the attack.

The agency had kept extensive records on Oswald's movements and had audio tapes of his time spent at the

Cuban consulate in Mexico City just weeks before the shooting. These tapes were suppressed by agents within the organization, much to FBI Director Edgar Hoover's dismay, who wrote in a memo on illegal CIA operations that he could not forget "the false story re Oswald's trip in Mexico."

According to the records, President Johnson, Deputy Attorney General Katzaenbach, and FBI Director Hoover decided to push forward the 'lone gunman theory' in an effort to suppress information about Oswald's connections to Cuba and the Kremlin. For geopolitical reasons, they feared making public information about his political connections. President Johnson told a senator that it had to be prevented "from kicking us into a war that can kill forty million Americans in an hour."

The last remaining closed files relating to the assassination—including information about the CIA operative who monitored Oswald, and sworn testimony from dozens of intelligence officials—must be released by 2017 unless certified as justifiably closed by the president of the United States.

Considering the lasting controversy surrounding the assassination, the new documents will undoubtedly raise a fresh round of discussion if and when released. If they aren't, many in the public sphere will read it as a sure sign of a cover-up and the conspiracy theories will persist.

PARDON ME?

TAKING A LOSS FOR LOYALTY

The Watergate scandal, erupted from the break-in at the Democratic National Committee offices on June 17, 1972, enraged the nation and rocked the political establishment to its core. President Nixon fought a two-year battle with the news media, the US Senate, the House of Representatives, and the Supreme Court in order to distance himself from responsibility. Though he tried to convince them otherwise, the American public believed he was trying to use the prestige and power of the presidential office to obstruct justice.

Nixon resigned the presidency when it became clear he would not survive a full impeachment and his vice president, Gerald Ford, took office. One month after Nixon resigned, Ford announced his decision to pardon the former president on a Sunday, hoping that the offbeat time would minimize the political fallout. No amount of evasion could quiet the fury of the American public and media who wanted to put Nixon on trial for his crimes. The ensuing controversy cost Ford the re-election, and after 28 months of serving as president of the United States he faded into obscurity, known only for his pardon of one of the most infamous men to ever take the Oval Office.

IN TOO DEEP

BUMBLING CREW OF CROOKS

"The American Dream has run out of gas," wrote British novelist J.G. Ballard following the Watergate scandal. "The car has stopped. It no longer supplies the world with its images, dreams, its fantasies. No more. It's over. It supplies the world with its nightmares now: the Kennedy assassination, Watergate, Vietnam."

Some say that no other Presidential scandal has sacrificed the trust of Americans more than the abuse of power by the Nixon administration. Facing a tough Democratic Party in his bid for re-election, Nixon concocted a scheme to spy on and intimidate the rival party. To make matters worse he tried to use every ounce of political clout he had as president to cover up the mess when it was discovered.

The scandal began on June 17, 1972, when Bernard Barker, Virgilio Gonzalez, Eugenio Martinez, James McCord, and Frank Sturgis were arrested for breaking and entering at the Democratic National Committee's headquarters in Washington.

CREEPS

Barker, Gonzalez, Martinez, McCord, and Sturgis were sent to the Watergate complex by G. Gordon Liddy, general counsel to the Committee for the Re-Election of the President (CRP). Earlier in the year Liddy presented an intelligence plan that involved extensive illegal activities including bugging the DNC's office and copying personal documents.

Although it was originally viewed as unrealistic, the CRP decided to move forward with the plan two months later as Nixon's popularity declined over the Vietnam War. After two successful break-ins at the Watergate Complex, CRP had tapped two phones in the DNC office and were getting good information. Seeking more dirt, a third break-in was ordered. The five men sent to the Watergate Complex were discovered by security guard Frank Wills.

Within hours of their arrest, the FBI discovered that one of the burglars was a Republican Party security aide and another had received a check for $25,000 for the Nixon reelection campaign. Further investigation revealed the CRP had spent thousands more on travel expenses for the men arrested.

The news media smelled a rat and ran with the story. Investigative pieces in the *Washington Post*, *Time*, and the *New York Times* relied on anonymous sources, including the infamous Deep Throat, for information that suggested the break-in was tied directly to the White House.

Among the reporters to cover the story were the Post's Bob Woodward and Carl Bernstein. Many of their leads came from Deep Throat whom they met on multiple occasions in an underground garage somewhere in Rosslyn, Virginia, at 2 a.m.

Richard Nixon declared "war on drugs" in June of 1971. Economist Jeffrey A. Miron published a study concluding that the annual savings on enforcement and incarceration costs from ending the war on drugs would be an estimated $41.3 billion.

PANIC SETS IN

Nixon was knee-deep in a political quagmire and desperate to squash the situation. On April 30, 1973, Nixon called for the resignation of H.R. Haldeman and John Ehrlichman, two of his presidential aides, as well as Attorney General Richard Klendienst. He also fired White House Counsel John Dean, who later testified before the Senate Watergate Committee that conversations in the Oval Office were taped.

Independent Special Prosecutor Archibald Cox, appointed to investigate the events surrounding the Watergate break-in, issued a supoena to President Nixon on Friday, October 19, 1973, asking for copies of the taped conversations in the White House. The President refused to comply.

The next day is known as the Saturday Night Massacre. Nixon went on a rampage and tried to fire Cox from his position. He ordered Attorney General Elliot Richardson to fire Cox. Richardson refused and resigned his post in protest. Nixon then ordered Deputy Attorney General William Ruckelshaus to fire Cox. Ruckelshaus also refused and resigned his post in protest. Finally, Nixon

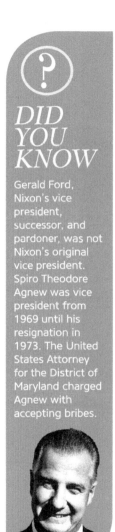

DID YOU KNOW

Gerald Ford, Nixon's vice president, successor, and pardoner, was not Nixon's original vice president. Spiro Theodore Agnew was vice president from 1969 until his resignation in 1973. The United States Attorney for the District of Maryland charged Agnew with accepting bribes.

DEEP THROAT

In 2005, Deep Throat was revealed to be former FBI Associate Director Mark Felt (above). For over thirty years his identity had remained a secret. His identity was revealed in a Vanity Fair article written by John D. O'Connor.

ordered Solicitor General Robert Bork to fire Cox. Bork complied and removed Cox from his post.

Congress was infuriated by Nixon's actions, and public indignation at Nixon reached an all time high. Less than a week after the incident, NBC News revealed that a majority of US citizens supported the impeachment of Nixon.

Amidst pressure from an angry public and an accusatory media, Nixon finally released transcripts of the tapes on April 29, 1974. The transcripts, of course, implicated the President and his aides.

The *Chicago Tribune*, which had supported Nixon, wrote, "He is humorless to the point of being inhumane. He is devious. He is vacillating. He is profane. He is willing to be led. He displays dismaying gaps in knowledge. He is suspicious of his staff. His loyalty is minimal."

The final straw that broke the back of Nixon's presidency came on August 5, 1974, when the White House released an audio tape recorded on June 23, 1972, just days after the break-in. It documented the initial stages of the cover-up and revealed

Right: October 21, 1973, Protesters parade in front of the White House with signs calling for the impeachment of President Nixon.

Senator George McGovern (D-SD) reads the newspaper headline of President Nixon's resignation, Aug. 7, 1974.

that Nixon was directly involved in its planning, going so far as to deliberately obstruct the investigation of the FBI.

On the tape, H. R. Haldeman can be heard informing Nixon that the FBI investigation "goes in some directions we don't want it to go," and suggests that Nixon "have Walters [CIA] call Pat Gray [FBI] and just say, 'stay the hell out of this. . . . this is business here we don't want you to go further on it."

Nixon approved the plan, saying "Good. Good deal. Play it tough. That's the way they play it and that's the way we are going to play it."

The release of the final tape destroyed any chance Nixon had of avoiding impeachment. The 10 congressmen who had previously voted against all articles of impeachment in the House Judiciary Committee announced that they would support impeachment when the motion was taken to the House floor, and on the night of August 7, 1974, Nixon was informed the all his support in Congress had disappeared.

The next evening President Richard Nixon resigned from office in a nationally televised address:

In all the decisions I have made in my public life, I have always tried to do what was best for the Nation . . . I have felt it was my duty to persevere, to make every possible effort to complete the term of office to which you elected me. . . . However, it has become evident to me that I no longer have a strong enough political base in the Congress to justify continuing the effort. Therefore, I shall resign the Presidency effective noon tomorrow.

Nixon later wrote of leaving the White House for the last time:

I found myself thinking not of the past, but of the future. . . . What could I do now?

OCTOBER SURPRISE

A SIDE DEAL WITH TERROR

During the 1980 presidential campaign between Jimmy Carter and Ronald Reagan, 52 Americans were being held hostage in Tehran, the Iranian capital. Carter worked hard to free them and even sent a covert military mission to Iran. Carter and Reagan both knew that if the hostages were released before Americans went to the polls, Carter would be assured of a second term.

Just 20 minutes after Carter's loss to Reagan the hostages were released, causing many to speculate that back-door negotiations had been taking place between the Reagan camp and Tehran to keep the hostages detained until after the election. The account has been supported by high-level officials in the Iranian and Israeli governments as well as by members of Reagan's staff and National Security Council member Gary Sick. Initially dismissed as conspiracy theory, the October Surprise scandal has now been all but accepted by historians.

US President Ronald Reagan listens as Bruce Laingen, top diplomatic hostage during the Iran hostage crisis, speaks at the offical welcome ceremony at the White House in Washington, D.C., Tuesday, January 27, 1981. On January 20, Iran released the 52 remaining hostages held at the US Embassy in Tehran for 444 days.

REAGAN'S REIGN

INTENT AND IMPACT COLLIDE

Ronald Reagan's presidency looms over the Republican Party as its highest achievement. His legacy is still so imminent throughout the party that contemporary nomination seekers regularly try to out-Reagan one another. Even Democratic opponents compare themselves to his high standard as a way to establish their statesman credentials. Still, is it possible that there was a man with the kind of presence that could hold the highest office in America and unite both Republicans and Democrats under one common goal?

Reagan (aka The Jellybean Man, named for his favorite snack) could not escape scandals at home or abroad.

News of corruption and graft in the Housing and Urban Development (HUD) office broke as Reagan was exiting the office. His administration had argued for years to cut back on the funding for various projects associated with the department, including home financing that was backed by the state and HUD-backed home insurance for those at risk.

When Congress refused to end the programs, administration officials reportedly retaliated by making little effort to regulate the distribution of funds that flowed through it. More than four billion dollars were wasted, and thousands of poor American families suffered.

HUD was not the only domestic scandal to tar Reagan's legacy. During his presidency AIDS moved from a little understood disease to a full-blown health crisis that killed nearly 21,000 Americans. His response was slow and, many contend, driven by conservative religious ideology rather than humanitarian public policy.

As the scandals piled up at home, Reagan's international policy was proving to be less than idealistically oriented as well.

MY ENEMY, MY FRIEND

Reagan supported the Contras in Nicaragua—anti-communist rebel groups who used military force to oppose the rise of the Socialist Party in that country.

At that time, Iran was involved in a bloody ground war with Iraq and badly needed weapons. Despite Iran having taken American government and military personnel hostage during (Reagan's predecessor) President Jimmy Carter's administration, Reagan's administration struck a secret deal with the Anti-American terrorist regime. America was to provide weapons for cash in order to fund Nicaraguan Contras, an illegal workaround since

Congress had denied the president funding. The program directly contradicted Reagan's campaign promise to never partner with terrorists.

By the time the transaction was discovered, 1,500 missiles had been shipped to Iran, and $30 million had been paid to the US government. Attorney General Edwin Meese discovered that $12 million had been diverted to arms sales to the Contras of Nicaragua.

Reagan initially denied any knowledge of the deal but the scandal did not go away. As evidence continued to emerge, it became obvious that Reagan had been involved. Finally, on March 4, 1987, he took to the airwaves: "A few months ago I told the American people I did not trade arms for hostages. My heart and my best intentions still tell me that's true, but the facts and the evidence tell me it is not."

NOT AS HONEST AS WE'D HOPED

"Debategate," a retroactive scandal that was discovered years into the Reagan presidency, unveiled that the president was not the paragon of moralism he presented himself as. Somehow Reagan's campaign staff obtained a copy of Jimmy Carter's, Reagan's then Democratic rival's, briefing book for the only televised debate between the two candidates. The cache also contained Carter's personal schedule and hundreds of other pages of strategy documents from the campaign.

Despite concerted efforts by the FBI and a congressional subcommittee to root out how Reagan obtained the documents, both reported that they had failed to determine the matter and the investigation was dropped.

Republican presidential candidate Ronald Reagan speaks to reporters following a tour of the Campbell Works. Reagan expressed shock as he visited the abandoned portions of the steel plant.

Despite several major policy scandals, many of which were outright illegal, Reagan's reputation survived and he has been written into the history books as one of the United States' most admired presidents. This was partly because his predecessor's administration was so unloved. But Reagan also possessed an asset that few politicians can genuinely claim: charm. The combination of his personal qualities, his party's unfailing efforts to enshrine his legacy, and the rise of Christian fundamentalism during his tenure has effectively ensconced Reagan as a president for the ages.

BILL, BEFORE AND AFTER

Bill Clinton exited the presidency as one of the most accomplished Presidents to hold the office. Still, despite a red-hot economy, balanced budget, record employment numbers, and a stellar foreign policy record, a brutal final term saw Clinton become the second President in American history to stand impeachment. Clinton took it in stride.

"BOY GOVERNOR"

1978
Elected Governor of Arkansas at age 32

CLINTON ☆ GORE
NEW LEADERSHIP IN '92

Clinton wins 1992 election over incumbent George H.W. Bush

Gennifer Flowers

Alleges affair with Clinton during 1992 presidential campaign

Clinton signs the Balanced Budget Act in 1995

1992
President Bill Clinton plays saxophone on the Arsenio Hall show

1997

"I'VE NEVER HAD SEXUAL RELATIONS WITH MONICA LEWINSKY"

1998
Impeached by the House of Representatives on two charges

ACQUITTED 1999

1998
"I DID HAVE A RELATIONSHIP WITH MISS LEWINSKY"

DOUBLE TROUBLE

GEORGE TIMES TWO

The 1988 presidential campaign between George H. W. Bush, Reagan's vice president, and Democratic nominee Michael Dukakis has been described as one of the nastiest in modern times.

Bush was a milquetoast candidate faced with a sinking economy. Dukakis commanded a populist appeal and the benefits of a voting public tired of Republican policy. With the deck seemingly stacked against their candidate, the Republican Party unleashed a tidal wave of negative advertising. The most infamous television spot featured convicted murderer Willie Horton.

Above: Former President George H.W. Bush, then first lady Laura Bush, then President George W. Bush, and former first lady Barbara Bush wave to reporters outside St. John's church in Washington.

Horton, an African American from Massachusetts, was furloughed for a weekend as part of a prison rehabilitation program. While temporarily freed, he raped a woman and violently assaulted her fiancé. The Bush campaign used the horrific incident to paint Dukakis as soft on crime. The ad was effective in two ways: it stoked conservative racism and drove many moderate voters away from the polls because of its distastefulness.

The ad, as well as many Dukakis missteps, helped Bush take the lead and secure victory.

A WARTIME LAME DUCK

Initially, Bush Sr.'s presidency was one of the most respected in the history of the country. When Iraq invaded Kuwait, Bush was able to put together an international coalition that repelled the invaders and largely diminished Saddam Hussein's position as a power broker in the Middle East. After a month of intense air raid attacks, a ground invasion pushed towards Kuwait City and captured Iraqi forces in less than 100 hours. His approval ratings skyrocketed as the coalition victory elevated US prestige abroad, and helped secure a Palestinian-Israeli peace conference.

Despite the unprecedented military victory, Bush, Sr. lost his re-election bid to the Governor of Arkansas William "Bill" Clinton in 1994. Clinton ran a successful campaign criticizing Bush for being out of touch with the working man—summed up by the memorable slogan, "It's the economy stupid." It was only after Bush, Sr. left office, in October of 1994, that a scandal broke out surrounding his appointment for US Treasurer, Catalina Vasquez Villalpando.

A criminal probe launched by the Department of Justice found that she received more than $167,000 from Communications International, Inc. (CII) a Georgia-based company she had previously headed. In addition, she held between $250,000 and $500,000 in company stock, which she did not disclose in her forms for nomination. CII, it turns out, had received 56 non-competitive contracts, totaling $68.6 million, between 1989 and 1992, when Villalpando served as Treasurer. Convicted of tax evasion, conspiracy to make false statements regarding her finances, and obstruction of a grand jury, she spent four months in jail for her crimes.

Bush, Sr. was also criticized for his pro-corporate policy decisions relating to the North American Free Trade Agreement (NAFTA) and financial services industry deregulation. NAFTA was seen as an erosion of America's manufacturing strength by the Democrats and FS deregulation would create the conditions that led to the 2007–8 financial crisis.

"DUBYA" TAKES CONTROL

In 2000 George W. Bush, son of Bush, Sr. and then Governor of Texas, defeated Vice President Al Gore and assumed office. Before his administration even moved in, he was already mired in controversy. The election was incredibly close, and a long battle over vote counts went all the way to the US Supreme Court.

The so-called "hanging chad" controversy started over the Florida voter count, where Bush won by a margin of only 537 votes. At the time many Florida voters used punched card ballots. When not pushed hard enough the machines did not create a hole in the ballot the tabulating machines relied on to count votes. A hand recount was called because of the thin margin separating the candidates. The Supreme Court controversially ruled that the manual recount was unconstitutional because different standards of counting were used in different counties. Bush, a champion of limited federal power, was saved by the federal apparatus his father had a hand in crafting.

Bush was awarded the presidency and controversy over the "stolen election" continues to this day. And with that beginning, Bush, Jr.'s presidency was destined to be more tumultuous than his father's.

HISTORY'S ACTOR

On September 11, 2001, hijacked commercial airline planes were crashed into New York City's twin towers, the Pentagon, and a field in western Pennsylvania, killing nearly three thousand people and plunging the nation into chaos. The largest attack on US soil since Pearl Harbor, 9/11 proved to be a major turning point in the United States' history.

Framing his response as the "War on Terror," the Bush administration initially rallied a coalition force to attack

FOUND OUT

IN 2002, Bush administration officials, including Vice President Dick Cheney, shared the identity of CIA operative Valerie Plame with conservative journalist Robert Novak. Novak later published the information in a syndicated column.

Friday, July 4, 2008, President Bush makes remarks during the annual Independence Day celebration and naturalization ceremony at Monticello, the historic home of Thomas Jefferson in Charlottesville, Virginia.

and remove al-Qaeda from Afghanistan where much of the 9/11 planning took place. The invasion immediately proved problematic due to the decentralized nature of the Afghan government and strong anti-American sentiment in the population.

Undeterred, Bush extended the war to encompass the destruction of terrorist ideology; he stated it "will not end until every terrorist group of global reach has been found, stopped and defeated." He noted the War on Terror is "a task that does not end."

The open-endedness of the Bush administration's policies set off alarms in the international community as well as domestically. Bush used the War on Terror to promote and defend concepts such as unilateralism, preemptive war, and the advocacy of torture. It was also his justification for invading Iraq in pursuit of terrorists.

Richard N. Haass, president of the Council on Foreign Relations, publicly criticized the invasion of Iraq, saying, "The decision to attack Iraq in March 2003 was discretionary: it was a war of choice. There was no vital American interests in imminent danger and there were alternatives to using military force, such as strengthening existing sanctions."

ME AGAINST THE WORLD

Bush set the tone for his administration late in 2001 when he said, "You're either with us or you are with the terrorists." It became difficult to tell who was who a short time later when it was reported that US soldiers and CIA operatives tortured, raped, sodomized, and murdered Iraqis and others at Abu Ghraib, a military prison in Baghdad.

The most stunning evidence was American soldiers' own photographs which were broadcast on CBS's 60 Minutes II, broadcast in April of 2004. The pictures rocked the world as rumors and conjecture of the United States' use of torture became reality. These photos showed Iraqi detainees naked with hoods over their heads, Iraqis piled naked on top of each other in a human pyramid. In one, Private Lynndie England gives a thumbs up and points at the genitals of a young Iraqi standing completely naked save for a sandbag over his head.

The administration tried to portray the abuse as an isolated incident but was quickly contradicted by reports from the Red Cross, Amnesty International, and Human Rights Watch. Further investigation revealed that Abu Ghraib was just one of many sites at which the United States was using torture to gain information from suspects. In 2008, despite public outcry for an end to the abuse of political prisoners, Bush opted to keep Guantanamo Bay, a naval base and detention center in Cuba open.

A HOUSE OF CARDS

In 2005 the evidence that was first used to justify the invasion of Iraq was found to have been completely fabricated. Rocco Martino, an occasional Italian spy known to peddle in forgeries, turned out to be the administration's sole source of information relating to Iraq's attempt to purchase ore that was used in the refinement of nuclear weapons.

On the domestic front, the War on Terror saw a rise in civilian surveillance in the form of the Terrorist Surveillance Program, a policy that, for the first time in the history of the country, provided for warrantless surveillance.

The American public was scandalized when the Bush administration confirmed that the NSA had license to eavesdrop on communications at home and abroad. Bush defended the program, stating that the authorization was "fully consistent" with his "constitutional responsibilities and authorities."

The Justice Department disagreed and on August 17, 2006, US District Judge Anna Diggs Taylor ruled the program

On May29, 2001 Jenna and Barbara Bush were cited by Texas police for underage drinking at a popular Tex-Mex restaurant in Austin. It was the second alcohol-related citation Jenna Bush had received in two months.

unconstitutional and illegal, and called for an end to unwarranted surveillance.

Bush has also been criticized for accepting no dissent in his Cabinet. On December 7, 2006, now known as the "Pearl Harbor Day Massacre," he fired nine US attorneys for political reasons. Attorney General Alberto R. Gonzalez insisted to Congress that he would never, ever make a change in a US attorney position for political reasons—the evidence proved otherwise. In Congressional hearings, David Iglesias of New Mexico, one of the fired prosecutors, said he felt "leaned on" in a certain investigation and said "I had a sick feeling in the pit of stomach," when he informed his superior he would not comply.

By the time Bush left office, his approval ratings were at an all-time low—just above 20 percent. In the six years since his presidency, his popularity has seen no rebound.

George W. Bush's presidency may very well go down in the history books as the most controversial ever. He ignored the rule of law, challenged political tradition, alienated allies, polarized the country, and even spurned his own party by refusing to choose a successor. To this day the Republican Party is trying to recover from Bush's time in office. Bush was largely acting on his own accord because nothing like the 9/11 attacks had ever happened. Ever the optimist, he wrote "It's too soon to say how many of my decisions will turn out," in his memoir, Decision Points.

CANDIDATES FOR CUBA

CURIOUS KINSHIP WITH COMMUNIST CUBA

1960 Fidel Castro, the president of the revolutionary state of Cuba, substantially raises taxes on American imports; Eisenhower retaliates by freezing Cuban assets in America, and lowering the import quota of Cuban sugar.

January 3, 1961 President Dwight D. Eisenhower closes the American Embassy in Havana and severs diplomatic relations after accusations from newly appointed Cuban President Fidel Castro that the The United States is using the embassy as a base for spies.

April 17, 1961 President John F. Kennedy sends approximately 1,400 Cuban exiles to overthrow Castro in the notoriously failed mission, the Bay of Pigs.

Above: Cuban refugees watching Kennedy on TV.

February 7, 1962 Kennedy announces complete embargo on Cuba which results in a loss of about $1.26 trillion over the next 50 years.

October 14–28, 1962 Cuban Missile Crisis. The United States discovers construction of a Soviet missile base in Cuba. Kennedy orders a naval blockade and the threat of nuclear war reaches seven minutes to midnight on the doomsday clock.

1966 President Lyndon B. Johnson passes Cuban Adjustment Act, inviting Cuban refugees who reach the United States the opportunity to gain citizenship.

April 15–October 31, 1980 President Jimmy Carter welcomes Cuban émigrés seeking asylum after an economic downturn on the island, spurring a mass exodus known as the Mariel Boatlift. All is well until Castro starts shipping inmates and mentally ill Cubans to the US border.

November 21 1999 President Clinton sends federal agents to retrieve Elian Gonzalez, a young Cuban boy, from a relative's home in Miami, only to send him back to Cuba.

2009 President Barack Obama eases travel and remittance restrictions to Cuba, allowing American citizens of Cuban descent to visit for religious and educational reasons.

December 17, 2014 President Obama orders the restoration of full diplomatic relations with Cuba after 18 months of secret negotiations with the help of Pope Francis, announcing the end of a stalemate that lasted over half a century.

PERIL
IN PROMISE

OBAMA SUPPORTERS
LEARN A HARD TRUTH

Barack Obama is the first African American to hold presidential office and the fourth president to be awarded the Nobel Peace Prize. He was a little-known senator from Chicago, Illinois who quickly captured the public's imagination with inspiring rhetoric and a compelling personal story. He ran an unusual campaign. It was optimistic and positive, a calculated strategy perfect for a country driven down by two wars and the endless controversies of the Bush presidency. The nation elected him with expectations of restoring peace and reason to government. America got the president it wanted but did not foresee the opposition he would receive once in office.

A NUMBER OF FIRSTS

Obama's campaign for presidential election in 2008 set fundraising records for the quantity of small donations from across the country. He is the first major-party presidential candidate to turn down public financing in the general election since its creation in 1976. Running on a platform that celebrated grass roots organizing, reform, and the need for change, Obama inspired a nation with his will to win—against all odds— the highest seat in the land.

Winning 52.9 percent of the popular vote and the heart of the nation, Obama inspired the public with his impassioned speeches and belief in a country that could change. "We recall that what binds this nation together is not the colors of our skin or the tenets of our faith or the origins of our names. What makes us exceptional—what makes us American—is our allegiance to an idea, articulated in a declaration made more than two centuries ago," said President Barack Obama, in his inauguration

SKY HIGH

The use of drones in military operations (like the above Puma aerial used in Afghanistan in 2013) has become a hot-button issue for Obama. The unmanned aerial vehicles have been used in several executions of terrorists that resulted in civilian deaths, in many instances including children.

speech on January 20, 2009. And with auspicious beginnings and a barrel of hope Obama strolled straight into history.

STUMBLING TOWARD FREEDOM

Obama's first act in office was to order the closing of the Guantanamo Bay Detention camp, a noble cause and a move he had promised in his campaign. Unfortunately Congress quickly undermined it. By refusing to appropriate the required funds, and preventing any Guantanamo detainees form entering the United States or foreign countries, the Republican opposition deftly flexed its power at the newly elected President.

In 2009 Obama issued a presidential memorandum formally closing the detention center and ordering the transfer of its prisoners to a correctional center in Thomson, Illinois. That plan was foiled when public officials disclosed that such a transfer would be illegal.

Two years later the President signed the Defense Authorization Bill, which restricts the transfer of Guantanamo prisoners to the mainland or foreign countries, directly interfering with his own plans to close the facility—he did promise to seek a repeal of those restrictions. No repeal was made and in 2012 The Authorization Bill was renewed.

The saga of Guantanamo continues. In 2015 it remains operational and houses at least 86 prisoners; restrictions on moving the prisoners have been signed into law each year. "This needs to be the year Congress lifts the remaining restrictions on detainee transfers and we close the prison at Guantanamo Bay—because we counter terrorism not just through intelligence and military action, but by remaining true to our Constitutional ideals, and setting an example for the rest of the world," Obama said during his State of the Union address in 2015.

Sadly, the circumstances surrounding the Guantanamo Bay controversy have been replicated in many other policies he has pursued.

GOOD HEALTH IS HARD TO COME BY

The Patient Protection and Affordable Care Act (PPACA) is a project Obama started in 2007. During his presidential campaign Obama promised quality, affordable, and portable health coverage for all. "Obamacare," as the PPACA has been dubbed, tries to do just that.

In the first few months of his presidency Obama called a joint session of Congress to construct a plan for healthcare reform. What ensued over the next few years was an all-out war between Republicans and Democrats with every single step of the arduous process becoming embroiled in debate. As the bill was crafted and prepped to hit the floor, Republican senators promised to filibuster it, described it as "unconstitutional," and have even taken the Health Care reform Act to the Supreme Court.

Signed into a law on March 23, 2010, after a grueling battle in both Congressional houses, Obamacare would take another two years to implement. Once the dust settled, it seemed as if Obama accomplished most of what he promised to achieve.

Obamacare expands Medicaid eligibility and offers cost assistance for buyers through health insurance marketplaces. It also mandates that every citizen in the United States have health care, or pay a 'shared responsibility' fee for each month they go without coverage. There have been many legal challenges to the law since PPACA signing. In *National Federation of Independent Business v. Sebelius*, the Supreme Court ruled that the individual mandate, requiring every citizen have health insurance, is constitutional, in a 5-4 split decision.

The court also found that individual states could not be forced to participate in the Medicaid expansion. Following the ruling, several traditionally Republican states, including Texas, Florida, Alabama, Wyoming, Arizona, Oklahoma, and Missouri have chosen to oppose all elements of Obamacare that they are able to.

Obamacare has also been the subject of three unsuccessful repeal efforts so far—from the Republicans in the 111th, 112th, and 113th Congresses—and Obama has promised to veto any bill that attempts to repeal the Act.

In 2013 House Republicans refused to fund the federal government, in an effort to delay the implementation of Obamacare. After Congress failed to pass a funding resolution by October 1st, the government shut down for 15 days. During the shutdown 800,000 government employees were indefinitely furloughed and 1.3 million worked without knowing when they would be paid. Under public pressure from the media and citizens, Republicans finally passed the budget on October 16, 2013, making this the third-longest government shutdown in US history.

While Republicans continue to fight the bill, claiming Obamacare will lead to a loss of 650,000 jobs, the immediate impact has yet to be determined. As of 2014, Insurance premiums rose 28 percent in 2013, compared to 26 percent in 2003, and the amount of workers paying deductibles over $1,000 doubled from what it was in 2008.

Considering the vitriol spilled in the media about Barack Obama, his presidency is sure to remain contentious long after he is gone from the White House. His detractors compare him to Hitler, claim he's not an American citizen, and are resolute in their attempts to repeal almost every major policy victory he has won. His supporters are coming to grips with the reality that politics in Washington can turn expectation into disappointment and resignation.

A PARTING
THOUGHT

"Character is like a tree and reputation like
a shadow. The shadow is what we think of it;
the tree is the real thing."
—ABRAHAM LINCOLN

SOURCES

History.com. "10 Things You May Not Know About Andrew Jackson."
March 14, 2014. Accessed May 2, 2015. www.history.com/news/10-things-you-may-not-know-about-andrew-jackson.

Mental Floss. "30 Presidential Nicknames, Explained." Accessed May 2, 2015.
mentalfloss.com/article/57009/30-presidential-nicknames-explained.

"1787-1800: Uproar over Senate Approval of Jay Treaty." Accessed May 2, 2015.
www.senate.gov/artandhistory/history/minute/
Uproar_Over_Senate_Treaty_Approval.htm.

Presidential Pet Museum. "Abraham Lincoln's Cats - Presidential Pet
Museum." January 9, 2014. Accessed May 2, 2015.
presidentialpetmuseum.com/pets/abraham-lincoln-cats/.

Los Angeles Times. "Areas Most in Need May Be Real HUD Scandal Victims."
July 2, 1989. Accessed May 2, 2015. articles.latimes.com/1989-07-02/news/mn-4888_1_hud-scandal.

"Barak Obama: The 50 Facts You Might Not Know." www.telegraph.co.uk
/news/worldnews/barackobama/3401168/Barack-Obama-The-50-facts-you-might-not-know.html.

LIFE. "Behind the Picture: Photos From the Night Marilyn Sang to JFK, 1962."
Accessed May 2, 2015. life.time.com/history/marilyn-monroe-john-kennedy-happy-birthday-may-1962/#1.

Bio.com. Accessed May 2, 2015. www.biography.com/people/george-washington-9524786#early-life-and-family.

CBSNews. "Clinton Cheated 'Because I Could'" Accessed May 2, 2015.
www.cbsnews.com/news/clinton-cheated-because-i-could-16-06-2004/.

Cowther, Linnea. "Ten Facts About Gerald Ford | Legacy.com." Ten Facts About
Gerald Ford | Legacy.com. Accessed May 2, 2015. www.legacy.com/news/
legends-and-legacies/ten-facts-about-gerald-ford/1074/.

Dreier, Peter. "Reagan's Real Legacy." Accessed May 2, 2015. www.thenation.
com/article/158321/reagans-real-legacy.

EconomicPolicyJournal.com. "LBJ: Paranoid, Narcissist, Bully, Sadist & Lout."
Accessed May 2, 2015. www.economicpolicyjournal.com/2013/01/
lbj-paranoid-narcissist-bully-sadist.html.

"First Lady Biography: Rachel Jackson." Rachel Jackson Biography.
Accessed May 2, 2015. www.firstladies.org/biographies/firstladies.
aspx?biography=7.

Haass, Richard N. (May–June 2013). "The Irony of American Strategy."
Foreign Affairs 92 (3): 58. Retrieved 26 June 2013.

Hersh, M. Seymour. "Torture at Abu Ghraib - The New Yorker." *The New Yorker.* Accessed May 2, 2015. www.newyorker.com/magzine/2004/05/10/torture-at-abu-ghraib.

Today I Found Out. "How A Donkey and an Elephant Came to Represent Democrats and Republicans." April 3, 2014. Accessed May 2, 2015. www.todayifoundout.com/index.php/2014/04/donkey-elephant-come-represent-u-s-political-parties/.

"How Mark Felt Became 'Deep Throat'" *Washington Post.* Accessed May 2, 2015. www.washingtonpost.com/politics/how-mark-felt-became-deep-throat/2012/06/04/gJQAlpARIV_story.html.

"How Thomas Jefferson and His Chef Brought French Cuisine to U.S." Tribunedigital-chicagotribune. October 3, 2012. Accessed May 2, 2015. articles.chicagotribune.com/2012-10-03/features/sc-food-0928-jeffer-son-20121003_1_jefferson-and-hemings-hemings-family-john-wayles.

Huebner, Lee. "The Checkers Speech After 60 Years." The Atlantic. September 22, 2012. Accessed May 2, 2015. http://www.theatlantic.com/politics/archive/2012/09/the-checkers-speech-after-60-years/262172/.

PBS. Interview: Annette Gordon-Reed." Accessed May 2, 2015. www.pbs.org/wgbh/pages/frontline/shows/jefferson/interviews/reed.html

CNN.com. "Jackie Kennedy's Pink Suit Locked Away from Public View" CNN. Accessed May 2, 2015. www.cnn.com/2013/11/21/us/jacqueline-kennedy-pink-suit/.

Kelly, Martin. "10 Things to Know About Franklin Pierce." Accessed May 2, 2015. americanhistory.about.com/od/franklinpierce/tp/10-Things-To-Know-About-Franklin-Pierce.htm.

Kelly, Martin. "Presidential Scandals." Accessed May 2, 2015. americanhistory.about.com/od/uspresidents/tp/presidential_scandals.htm.

Kom, Kim, and Special O. "How to Keep Your Private Information Safe." USA *Today.* January 12, 2014. Accessed May 2, 2015. www.usatoday.com/story/tech/columnist/komando/2014/01/12/private-informationsafe/4341481/.

Nilsson, Jeff. "The Long Tradition of the Smear Campaign." The *Saturday Evening Post* The Long Tradition of the Smear Campaign Comments. Accessed May 2, 2015. www.saturdayeveningpost.com/2012/08/25/history/post-perspective/tradition-dirty-politics.html.

Saloncom RSS. "Our Real First Gay President." Accessed May 2, 2015. www.salon.com/2012/05/14/our_real_first_gay_president/.

"Paternalism 2.0." The Economist. August 23, 2014. Accessed May 2, 2015.
www.economist.com/news/business/21613359-american-employers-
are-rethinking-their-role-workers-health-care-paternalism-20.

"Press Attacks." George Washington's Mount Vernon. Accessed May 2, 2015.
www.mountvernon.org/research-collections/digital-encyclopedia/
article/press-attacks/.

"Rachel Donelson Robards." Rachel Donelson Robards. Accessed May 2, 2015.
self.gutenberg.org/articles/Rachel_Donelson_Robards.

"Return to Normalcy | Teaching American History." Teaching American
History. Accessed May 2, 2015. teachingamericanhistory.org/library/
document/return-to-normalcy/.

Staff, NCC. "James Buchanan: Why is he considered America's worst
president?" Yahoo! News. Accessed May 2, 2015. news.yahoo.com/
james-buchanan-why-considered-america-worst-president-
100229629—politics.html.

Summers, Anthony (2013). Not in Your Lifetime. New York: Open Road. ISBN
978-1-4804-3548-3.

Swaine, Jon. "Barack Obama: The 50 Facts You Might Not Know."
The Telegraph. Accessed May 2, 2015. www.amazon.com/Not-
Your-Lifetime-Defining-Assassination/dp/1480435481.

"Teapot Dome Scandal | United States History." Encyclopedia Britan-
nica Online. Accessed May 2, 2015. www.britannica.com/EBchecked/
topic/585252/Teapot-Dome-Scandal.

"The Inauguration of George Washington, 1789." The Inauguration of George
Washington, 1789. Accessed May 2, 2015. www.eyewitnesstohistory.com/
washingtoninaug.htm.

"The Snowden Saga: A Shadowland of Secrets and Light." Vanity Fair.
Accessed May 2,2015. www.vanityfair.com/news/politics/2014/05/
edward-snowden-politics-interview.

"The Unexpected Death of President Harding, 90 Years Ago." History.com.
August 2, 2013. Accessed May 2, 2015. www.history.com/news/
the-unexpected-death-of-president-harding-90-years-ago.

"The XYZ Affair." The XYZ Affair. Accessed May 2, 2015.
www.john-adams-heritage.com/the-xyz-affair/.

"Troves of files on JFK assassination remain secret." BostonGlobe.com.
Accessed May 2,2015. www.bostonglobe.com/2013/11/25/

government-still-withholding-thousands-documents-jfk-
assassination/PvBM2PCgW1H11vadQ4Wp4H/story.html.

"Warren G. Harding – Scandals and illness." Accessed May 2, 2015.
www.presidentprofiles.com/Grant-Eisenhower/Warren-G-Harding-
Scandals-and-illness.html.

Yannielli, Joseph. "The Assassination of Zachary Taylor."
Digital Histories at Yale. Accessed May 2, 2015. histi3.commons.
yale.edu/2013/11/22/the-assassination-of-zachary-taylor/.

INDEX

CONTINUE THE
CONVERSATION

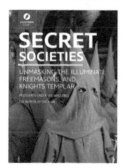

DISCOVER MORE AT
www.lightningguides.com/books

Also available as an eBook

CPSIA information can be obtained at www.ICGtesting.com
Printed in the USA
LVOW02s1344140915

453434LV00003B/3/P